Fly in the Buttermilk

Singular Lives

The Iowa Series in North American Autobiography

Albert E. Stone, Series Editor

ᴪ

University of Iowa Press

Iowa City

Fly in the Buttermilk

The Life Story of Cecil Reed

Cecil A. Reed with Priscilla Donovan

Foreword by Albert E. Stone

University of Iowa Press, Iowa City 52242

Printed in the United States of America

Design by Richard Hendel

Printed on acid-free paper

Library of Congress Cataloging-in-Publication Data

Reed, Cecil A., 1913–

    Fly in the buttermilk: the life story of Cecil Reed / by Cecil A.
Reed, with Priscilla Donovan; foreword by Albert E. Stone.

        p.   cm.—(Singular lives)

    ISBN 0-87745-415-9, ISBN 0-87745-416-7 (paper)

    1. Reed, Cecil, 1913– . 2. Legislators—Iowa—
Biography.   3. Afro-American legislators—Iowa—
Biography.   4. Iowa. General Assembly. House of
Representatives—Biography.   5. Iowa—Politics and
government. I. Donovan, Priscilla. II. Title. III. Series.

F621.R34   1993

977.7′00496073—dc20   93-18624

                                       CIP

97 96 95 94 93 C 5 4 3 2 1

03 02 01 00   P 8 7 6 5

Dedicated to

my late son, David,

Harold Hughes,

Joan Liffring-Zug,

Frank Nye, and

George Mills.

These people gave me the opportunity

to look beyond my little world.

"Communication is the way to friendship;

every facility for exchange of words, or personal

views, between people removes a stone in the walls

of provincial hatreds and prejudices."

—by an unknown blacksmith, 1840

Contents

Foreword *Albert E. Stone*

This autobiography, the eighth in Iowa's Singular Lives series, is only the second to come from someone raised in Iowa. Yet *Fly in the Buttermilk: The Life Story of Cecil Reed* could scarcely be more different from Ray A. Young Bear's 1992 *Black Eagle Child: The Facepaint Narratives*. To be sure, the black man from Cedar Rapids and the Mesquakie poet from Tama both reconstruct their minority experiences within—and against—the same heavily white midwestern society. However, Cecil Reed does so with the assistance of Priscilla Donovan. Their collaboration, far from unusual in this age of *The Autobiography of Malcolm X* and *Iacocca*, is in other respects a thoroughly traditional memoir. Rather than *generating* a self as Young Bear does in the imaginative act of writing, Reed and Donovan *authenticate* one historical experience within its social, political, and racial circumstances. By means of a chronological account stitched together by dates, names, places, photographs, and historical backgrounds, they reconstitute in words a consistent social self securely situated in recognizable social and temporal settings. The result, for all its authors' modest intentions and battery of conventional literary devices, is a classically patterned American success story.

The bare bones of Cecil Reed's narrative are in several respects as familiar as they are consoling to many potential readers. "For the most part," he remarks, "you'll not find sad, hopeless stories in this book because I'm a positive, hopeful man." This optimistic achiever began life as a cheerful child in a close-knit black/white/Native American family. Despite racism and modest resources, the Reeds created an admirable environment for their children; father and mother saw to it that the surrounding (and sometimes threatening) white worlds of Illinois, Nebraska, and Iowa didn't rob them of love, food, housing, work, music, fellowship. Cecil early learned the values of hard, skilled labor. This helped instill self-respect as it generated the respect of others. Though denied much formal education—like more famous success-storytellers such as Franklin and Malcolm X—he mastered a truly astonishing variety of jobs: newsboy, handyman, chef, floor finisher, dancer and singer, jukebox repairer, landlord, and motel owner. He ended as a prominent Cedar Rapids entrepreneur, chair of the Chamber of Commerce, and the first black Republican elected to the Iowa House of Representatives. Local and statewide success, smoothed by genuine friendliness and a calculated stylishness in dress, decorum, and speech, led to regional and national recognition. Among the many photographs documenting this rise is one showing Cecil Reed shaking hands with Richard Nixon. Thus the initial metaphor of self keying this autobiography—being a fly in the white buttermilk of the rural Midwest—is repeatedly revised as this proud but ingratiating fly relates experiences and achievements "inside" as well as "on the surface of" white America. A potentially demeaning image of self and race is thus defused and redefined.

Such a description of *Fly in the Buttermilk* suggests a book designedly appealing to several different audiences. Doubtless its chief readership will be older whites and blacks of the educated middle class, people sharing the upbeat, integrationist ethics of its subject and impressed by the notable names who have come under Cecil Reed's genial spell and who gave at least lip service to his ideals. But the memoir is also written to inform and inspire young readers. In fact, Reed's past includes writing one poignant poem, "What Do We Tell the Children?" Young people in particular, he hopes, will see how widely spread and deeply embedded in the American social and historical fabric blacks have been—*and* what common problems even such isolated black families in small midwestern cities share with brothers and sisters in Harlem, Chicago's South Side, and Watts. If younger blacks wince or sneer at Reed's "Guidelines" for getting along as a black in white America (*Be honest . . . Dress well, speak well . . . Keep a clean, neat home . . . Think of the needs of others . . . Be an interesting, well-informed person . . . Make your home an inviting place . . . Take an inch instead of a mile*), they may find themselves grudgingly granting Reed the right to address them as the parent of a son who, wounded to the quick by condescension, name-calling, and racial stereotyping, committed suicide. That's "the one roadblock I can't turn into a stepping-stone, the one scar I can't turn into a star." In fact, Reed's recollection of a long fight with David over a razor blade is unforgettable. It is the real-life equivalent of the scene in Alice Childress's *A Hero Ain't Nothing but a Sandwich* in which a black stepfather fights to save his addicted stepson on a snowy Harlem rooftop. The difference between the two selfless acts is that David Reed succeeded later in killing himself. Autobiographical truth here is more convincing than fictional—even when located in a narrative which in other respects reads like a Dale Carnegie how-to-succeed handbook.

How consciously Cecil Reed has understood and controlled his ascent is not always clear. Does he, for example, grasp the unreality of language like "the beautiful flower garden of colors we call the United States"? What do we make of a guide to interracial and intergenerational living who confesses that he's never been very clear as to goals or strategies? "During my brief stay in the House," he writes, "I learned so much, took in so much, it was almost frightening. I didn't try to figure out where it was going or how to organize it. Changes, opportunities, and problems were too many to be analyzed. I just trusted that there was some purpose, some higher reason for my being there. If I'd tried to plan or control the details, I might have limited the outcome."

Many autobiographers, of course, admit they did not understand what was happening to them in medias res. Even an intellectual as wise and self-reliant as W. E. B. Du Bois confesses in his *Autobiography* that "the world seized and whirled me." In retrospect, though, the greater autobiographers communicate later understanding of what they couldn't comprehend at the time. Knowledge and enlightenment, in such cases, frequently follow some decisive turning point, crisis, or conversion. In Cecil Reed's recollections, it isn't clear when or if such illumination has occurred. David's suicide is one possibility, and Reed's generalizing from his sensitive son's tragic fate to those of other young black Americans reveals a firm grasp of the realities which he himself— and perhaps others in his generation and situation—has avoided.

In one other episode, though, Reed identifies what may be a larger, more mysterious source of power and insight lying behind the fortuitous twists and turns of a successful career. Though a series of influential models (black and white men, chiefly) and a loving wife are fondly memorialized, these forces guiding his path seem to pale by comparison with a momentous experience he once had. "I was discouraged and worried," he admits during his Cedar Rapids career as small businessman and race leader.

> . . . every day had to be almost perfectly carried out because you had to think of making payroll, putting the workmen's compensation money in escrow, maintaining trucks and machines, and buying gas, oil, and supplies. Should I be spending what little free time I had making free speeches? . . .

I don't know whether I dozed or exactly what happened, but all of a sudden I heard a boom. The light around the motel became so bright it lit up the entire surrounding area. Suddenly this little guy just appeared before me. He was about 5 feet 9 or 10 with long black hair, very kind eyes, and an athletic build. There seemed to be a light around his head. . . .

. . . Then he looked me directly in the eye and said, "Don't worry, it will all work out. You are doing the right thing. Just keep making your speeches and doing everything you're doing, and you'll never have to worry about money again." Just like that he turned and walked away. . . . He went away, and the light went with him.

Though this vision or simple dream doesn't appear to organize or reorder Cecil Reed's life, values, or self-awareness, it affords, I believe, a striking glimpse inside the heart of this busy, good-hearted apostle of work, the profit motive, and American ideals of tolerance. Perhaps if it went further toward "explaining" the deeper coherence of this man's character and activities it would sound more falsely unconvincing than I think it does. For one thing, the nighttime encounter with "the nice little Jewish guy" anticipates the final metaphor of self with which Reed and his amanuensis end this autobiography. "Since then," he writes of retirement, "my life has been not as a fly in the buttermilk but more like a passenger on an airplane ride. When trouble or turbulence comes, you listen to the pilot and fasten your seat belt while you move above it. . . . Then when you hit another rough spot, rise on up again. . . . up . . . up . . . to 38,000 feet. When you get up there, seven miles high, you suddenly break through to where it's smooth and bright. . . . Free now, above the clouds. Free to look down and see our beautiful country so rich in diversity. Free to continue an endless mission to bring about harmony in a world of difference." This last homily rings truer, I think, to Cecil Reed's whole life than does the original figure of speech which gives his very American story its title.

Preface and Acknowledgments

When I was searching for a title for this book that would describe my singular experience in life, I thought of something my black friends used to laugh about when I was in a picture of my class or team and I was the only black. They would say, "You show up like a fly in the buttermilk." It seemed like the best title possible because I've been the fly in the buttermilk all my life and proud of it. I don't see flies or buttermilk as derogatory. Both have important roles to play. I know the flies did.

Thousands of us were raised in all-white neighborhoods and went to all-white schools where we were taught by white teachers. Whites were our role models. We walked the white streets and worked in a white work force. We lived through depressions and wars, racial strikes and riots, repression and murder, the Black Revolution and the Great Society. Since I was born into this situation, I thought little of it. Now that I am old, I realize how different my life was from most blacks'. I think that my experiences represent the experiences of other flies in the buttermilk. And I'd like others to know what we did and how we did it. As I look back, a part of me feels that being black in a white world was good for us and later for my family. After all, it was a true picture of our total society. In our nation of more than 250 million people, blacks are 12.5 percent of the population, Hispanics are 7 percent, American Indians less than 1 percent, and Asian-Americans will soon reach 3 percent. What I experienced prepared me to cope with reality.

A part of me, too, wants things to be different, easier for young blacks, low-income whites, and other suffering minorities. I hope this book will help them; I hope it will say thanks to those who helped me along the way.

I'd like to give special mention to a number of people.

Members of my family: my dear wife, Evelyn, and children, Carol, Dick, Mike, and Dave; my parents and siblings, Frances, Edith, and Lula, and Wally, Jim, and George.

Several men who were mentors and role models for me in my youth: George Niery, the blacksmith, Mr. Anderson, the insurance man, and Bob Vlach, chief of police.

Colleagues, associates, and friends: Bob Caldwell, executive secretary of the Chamber of Commerce, Bud Jensen, Tom Riley, John Ely, Bev Taylor, Rod Kenyon, Jim Gibson, Governor Robert Ray, Maurice Berringer, Chief of Police Benesh, Howard Hall, Judge and Wilma Glanton, Mrs. Gibson, John Estes, Bob Wright, Bob Moelhmon, Dr. Galen Dodge, Wayne Janssen, John Douglas, Ana May Weems, and Joan Liffring-Zug.

Friends in the clergy: Rev. Cleaver and Fathers Cassidy, Klien, and Stemm, as well as Sisters Sabastien, Clarice, and Eileen.

The six best secretaries anyone ever had: Jeanie Walker Mitchell for the many Reed enterprises, Sandy Yizer in the legislature, Alma Gerdus in Job Service, Betty Parrot in EEO, Mary Evans in Job Corps, and Kay Robinson in the Department of Labor.

The caring, talented staffs at the National Veterans Training Institute, University of Colorado at Denver, and the Office of Personnel Management in Oak Ridge, Tennessee, Lancaster, Pennsylvania, and Denver, Colorado; Iowa Governors Harold Hughes and Robert Ray and the wonderful, warm people of Iowa, particularly Cedar Rapids.

—Cecil Reed

Introduction

Probably every black person in the United States has a story to tell that could shed light upon this country's past and future. But Cecil Reed's story is the most compelling one I have come across . . . not because of the discrimination he has suffered or the problems he has conquered, although both abound in his life. Cecil's story is compelling because he speaks with love instead of anger, hope instead of despair, and wisdom instead of compulsion. Cecil's story is important because of the unique circumstances of his life and the fruitful ways he dealt with those circumstances. Keep in mind as you read this book that there was no Civil Rights Act until his fiftieth birthday. This means that for most of his life he could not count on being able to use a public restroom, restaurant, hotel room, or water fountain. Most of his life there were no equal employment rights, no affirmative action. It was almost unheard of during the first half of his life for a black to get a loan for a home, business, or schooling. Although Cecil was born more than fifty years after the Thirteenth Amendment to the Constitution "freed the slaves," social, economic, and political practices throughout his youth and adulthood ranged all the way from unthinking bias to blatant racism. In spite of all this, Cecil managed to lead a happy, fulfilling life.

Cecil's life is full of work and good works. He has held every conceivable kind of job—from shoe shining and tap dancing to being regional director of the U.S. Department of Labor's Manpower Commission. As the first black Republican legislator in the state of Iowa, he so moved his colleagues that they voted unanimously to pass a fair housing act. He has lived in the worlds of entertainment, federal bureaucracies, and state politics. He has been honored by presidents and spat upon by schoolchildren, but his message is positive, kind, practical, and humorous. And that message has been heard by hundreds of thousands of people across this country. He speaks with such honesty about real human issues that it is the rare person who is not touched by what Cecil has to say about life.

Cecil and I first met in 1987 when he came to speak on a regular basis at the University of Colorado at Denver. I was a course manager and teacher at the university's National Veterans Training Institute. When I wrote a story about him for the institute's newsletter, I realized that he had led a fascinating life. When he said he had twenty-nine notebooks full of notes, mementos, pictures, and letters about his life that he wanted to organize into some permanent form, I was hooked. I am by nature a "saver" and wanted to preserve his story.

I am also a journalist by training (Kent State University) and know a good story when I see one. As a published author since 1984 (*Whole-Brain Thinking* and *The Flexibility Factor*, coauthored with Jacquelyn Wonder), I was only *slightly* intimidated by the twenty-nine notebooks. We began working on the book every time he was in Denver. He taped his earliest memories, then we worked and reworked them. It is not easy to reconstruct your childhood. His story is as accurate as possible thanks mostly to the sharp memories of Cecil's sisters, Frances, who lives in Des Moines, Iowa, and Edie, in Cedar Rapids.

Most of the time though we'd go through his notebooks and talk about what he wanted to say. I'd get it on paper, and then, the next time he'd be in Denver, we'd review and revise what I'd written. Over the next five years there were many revisions—not because he'd changed his attitude about what he wanted to say, but because I didn't always get it right. But it became easier as we got to know each other better. Sometimes when we had upheavals in our lives such as health or family problems, we'd not write for several months. But neither of us ever gave up. We discovered that we both are "country folk," and this enabled us to work together easily, understand one another fully, and persist doggedly.

Most chapters chronicle a period in Cecil's life. Others are singular episodes, such as the suicide of his youngest son and the time he thinks he was visited by an angel. Some chapters are composites of experiences in traveling and in the entertainment world. All, I hope, do justice to this wise, caring man.

—*Priscilla Donovan*

1   Tangled Roots

"If you cut the throat of one of 'em, the others will smell blood and turn tail," the slaves on General Lee's plantation advised. They were talking to Ben, the slave who'd been chosen to take young Henry Lee to the West and out of slavery. They wanted Ben to know what to do if white bounty hunters sent bloodhounds after them on their perilous journey from Virginia to Illinois before the Civil War. Being hunted by bloodhounds was just one of the dangers Henry and Ben would encounter during the many weeks it took to thread their way across country, moving by night and hiding out by day.

This is a story told by my Grandpa Henry Lee about how he came to live in Illinois. He explained that he and his twin brother, Harry, were half-brothers of General Robert E. Lee, the brilliant military leader of the Confederacy. All three were sons of Henry "Light-Horse" Harry Lee, a distinguished cavalry commander in the American Revolution and a close friend of George Washington. Light-Horse Harry Lee was a member of the Continental Congress, a governor of Virginia, a leader in suppressing the Whiskey Rebellion in 1794, and a United States congressman from 1799 to 1801.

Light-Horse Lee had an equally busy personal life. He was a compulsive gambler who lost most of his family's fortune. Therefore, General Lee grew up in genteel poverty in Alexandria, Virginia. His half-brothers, Henry and Harry Lee, were born to one of Light-Horse Lee's house slaves. Henry looked white and his twin, Harry, looked black.

Henry was probably sent away from the plantation out of a genuine concern for his welfare, not because he was so light. In fact, slavemasters often purposely bred light-skinned children to work in the houses because they were more acceptable to whites. At any rate, he was placed in the care of a slave and sent west from the Lee plantation to live as a free man in Illinois.

In old age, Henry Lee told this story many times to his step-grandchildren, my older sisters and brother. Grandpa Lee was the second husband of my grandmother, Sarah Mitchell Lee. I was born one year after he died in 1912.

My Story Begins

Some people in Collinsville, Illinois, might have doubted that Grandpa Henry Lee was the half-brother of General Robert E. Lee and the son of Light-Horse Harry Lee, but there was plenty of physical evidence to support his claim. In the first place, Grandpa Lee was nearly white and *looked* like the Lees. Second, the fact that Light-Horse Lee was named both Henry and Harry seems more than coincidental to the black and white half-brothers being named Harry and Henry. Third, regular as a clock, Grandpa Lee got a monthly check from Virginia which he said was given to him because he was a Lee. Fourth, Grandpa Lee was a landowner and never worked for anyone else— a nearly impossible status for an Illinois Negro at the turn of the century. Some freed slaves owned land during that period through home-steading, but none of them had money to live on. They had to work desperately hard to build a home, plant crops, and buy farm animals.

"Free" as whites then or now understand the word is vastly different from the kind of freedom slaves who came west during that time actually experienced. Some were runaways and some had tenuous claims to having earned their freedom, but none of them had the comfortable life that Grandpa Lee enjoyed. He bought a farm outright in Collinsville. It had four houses. He and Grandma Lee lived in the big house, and other relatives lived in the smaller ones. They all worked the farm together, mainly grow-ing produce to sell in East St. Louis (near Collinsville), as well as hogs and chickens.

When Grandma and Grandpa Lee met, she was a widow with six children, one of whom was Julia, my mother. Grandma's first husband, my blood grandfather, was also named Henry, Henry Jones. But he was a dark black man from Madagascar. Grandma was a lighter black. She and Grandpa Lee were married in 1892 and had one child together. Grandma Lee died at the age of 102 in Davenport, Iowa.

I remember Grandma Lee best for the stories she told about the old days. My sister Frances and I would sit at her feet by her old steamer trunk and she'd show us her wedding dress and script money from the Civil War. The trunk was filled with packages, each wrapped in cloth and tied with ribbon. One was the license for her marriage to Grandpa Lee. It had red hearts in each corner and little cherubs at the top. Another held Grandpa Lee's dis-charge from the Civil War. It was printed or painted on oilcloth and signed by General Ulysses S. Grant.

Grandma Lee is shown here at 101. She died a year later in Davenport. She was born Sarah Ann Mitchell in Waterloo, Illinois, in 1858. She once saw Abraham Lincoln. By her first husband, Henry Jones, she had six children, one of whom was my mother, Julia. She had one child by her second husband, Henry Lee, a half-brother to General Robert E. Lee.

On the left is Frances, my oldest living sister, who remembers Grandpa Lee's stories about coming west from the Virginia plantation where he was born to a slave and the father of General Robert E. Lee. On the right is my sister Laura, at age seven. She died when she was sixteen, before I was born. George, my oldest brother, is shown in the middle.

Dad's Side of the Family

My father, William Garrett Reed, was the son of Grandpa John Reed, who was born in Ireland. Grandpa's mother died when he was born, so his father's family (Aunt Maggie and her husband, Harry Kennedy) brought him along with his three sisters—Lettie, Lutricia, and Laura—with them to the United States in 1837, and they settled in St. Louis. Harry opened a store, and Grandpa Reed worked there until he was seventeen. Then he got a job as a stevedore on a boat that went to all the Indian trading posts along the Mississippi River. When Grandpa Reed was at an Indian village near Davenport, Iowa, he saw a beautiful Indian maiden, Francine Felice Butcher, and took her to Collinsville. She was the daughter of Chief John Butcher, a Blackhawk Indian.

Grandpa and Grandma Reed had nine children, five of whom survived: Robert, Kenneth, George, Lucy, and William Garrett. My father was the youngest, and his mother, Francine, died during his birth. This left Grandpa Reed to raise an infant (my dad) and four other children. Grandpa Reed then married a white English woman, Florence, who bore two children and died at the birth of the second. His third wife, Suphrona, a black woman, had twelve boys and three girls by him: Taft, Roosevelt, Jackson, Nelson, Jefferson, William, Grant, Ulysses, Thomas, Adam, John, Van Bruan, Lucy, May, and Clara. That meant that my father, W. G. Reed, was one of twenty-two siblings.

You'll read more about both my parents' siblings throughout the book, but basically, we lost track of these step-relatives. Most of them had light complexions and could hold jobs usually reserved for whites. Several of them lived in Chicago and worked for the fancy department stores.

Except for those women who died during childbirth, people on my dad's side of the family were pretty long-lived: Grandpa Reed died at 114, Chief Butcher at 123, and Grandpa Reed's sisters at 104, 107, and 109.

First of the Flies

These tangled family lines illustrate a few realities of life in those times: the high death rate of women during childbirth and the equally high incidence of white men intermingling their blood with blacks and Indians. Karl Gunnar Myrdal, an economics professor at the University of Stockholm who shared the 1974 Nobel Prize for economics (the first ever) and was executive secretary of the United Nations Economic Commission for Europe (1947–1957), made an exhaustive study of the black population in the United States in the early forties. In his book, *An American Dilemma: The Negro Problem and Modern Democracy*, published in 1944, Myrdal estimated that at least 70 percent of blacks in this country had white blood in their veins. He described how slave traders in Africa and slaveholders in the United States purposely bred mulattoes because they were more acceptable as house slaves and because mulatto women were considered more attractive as sex objects.

Another reality of slavery is that people not in charge of their lives have a difficult time keeping track of family history. Official records of slave families were not kept except, perhaps, as entries in plantation ledgers. Although Indians had strong oral histories of family lineages, once they were pawns in the westward movement, many of their traditions disappeared, too.

The picture for blacks in the West was especially confusing. Some were free because they'd served in the war, some had been freed by their owners, some were runaways, some were indentured servants, and some were slaves in the traditional sense. The status of blacks in the West changed, however, even for those who came as traditional slaves. Frontier life was so rugged that many white families stayed behind until houses were built, so white and black men lived and labored shoulder to shoulder in the first migrations. Then when the white families arrived on the scene, social separatism set in again. Even though slavery status returned for some blacks, it was never quite the same. Once you've been so dependent on one another for survival, your attitude changes. White men (and some women) in the West had a different experience with blacks than did those in the rest of the country. Spread throughout the emerging West in many different life-styles, blacks were respected and tolerated for their skills and energies, which were so desperately needed. Many of them became successful entrepreneurs and leaders in every area of frontier life.

Even in such extraordinary circumstances, Grandpa Lee's situation was unique. His heritage made it possible for him to have a financial head start, which in turn enabled his step-family to live in the plains states and to become some of the first flies in the buttermilk in the West.

2 **P**icnics and Real Cowboys

I was born on October 23, 1913, in Collinsville, Illinois, to W.G. and Julia Reed. My parents had eight children—Laura, George, Frances, Lulu Bell, Wallace, James, Edith, and me. One of the first things I remember about Collinsville is the song all the kids used to sing when we went to Forest Park. "Hark, hark, the dogs do bark. We're on our way to Forest Park." It was a beautiful green spot where families would go after church on Sunday for a picnic. Collinsville was segregated in those days, but blacks had free access to some parks, lakes, and rivers for swimming and picnicking.

Parks then weren't like they are today. Most of them were acreages set aside for recreation, but there were no restrooms, picnic tables, or shelters. You changed into your swimming clothes in the bushes. The grown-ups kept watch to make sure boys and girls didn't peek at each other.

There'd be twenty or thirty of us riding in an old flatbed, horse-drawn wagon with baskets of food and mason jars of lemonade. The children and men would play ball, wade in the water, and play catch while the women would spread the food out on blankets. Another favorite with the men was pitching horseshoes. They'd use a spike made from an axle and keep grease on it so it wouldn't rust. You'd hear them betting on who was going to win. They'd call out, "It's a leaner, it's a ringer." But mostly I stuck around the women fixing food. They'd give me samples all the while they were chatting away.

All through the warm afternoons we'd sing church songs and romp in the park. On the way home there'd be more singing while many tired heads nodded off as we snuggled in the hay that covered the wagon bed. Lots of times, you'd wake up in bed and not know how you got there.

I used to lie in the grass and look at the sky or watch the sunlight flicker in the bushes. I'd wonder where the water came from in the pond we swam in. It seemed like a huge pond to me but probably wasn't much more than a big puddle. Today it's cemented in and is only a wading pool. I remember wearing cutoff bib overalls. My mother used to scrub those overalls on washboards until she'd turn the pockets and wear-spots white. We were always kind of ashamed of them once they looked so faded and worn. But today they'd call them acid-washed, give them a designer name, and charge you $90 for them. Mom also used to scrub us down pretty good with P&G soap . . . sometimes it was enough to turn you white.

William Garrett Reed, my father, was called W.G. by most everyone who knew him. He was half American Indian and half white. He was born on August 11, 1876, in Collinsville, Illinois. He died in Cedar Rapids at age eighty in 1957. He was 6 feet tall and had black hair and red whiskers.

Red Whiskers

As is common with little children, my parents were the most important people in my life. Dad was a big, strong guy with a lot of determination. He was part Irish and part American Indian, so he had red whiskers and black hair. He shaved every day of his life because he didn't like the looks of those red whiskers. I don't

Julia Elizabeth Jones, my mother. She was much darker than this picture indicates. Both of her parents were black. She was 5 feet tall but always dressed in a way that made her seem taller. She was born in 1881 and died February 18, 1951.

know why, unless it was because he was a "half-breed," a term used in those days for someone who was half Indian and half Caucasian. Add to that the fact that he was married to a woman with black blood.

Until I started writing this book, I gave no thought to my dad's heritage. He was my dad. Mom was dark and Dad was light—not an uncommon thing. I was accustomed to seeing many different colors in black families, and I really never paid attention to the composition of white families. But apparently whites noticed! When Dad would go to a new job or new situation, people automatically assumed he was white. This led to some sticky situations—which were sometimes funny, too. Once, when we were all going to Davenport, Dad got on the train first and sat in the regular car with all the other passengers. No one paid any attention to him until the rest of the family joined him. When the conductor (always white in those days) saw five black children and my mother sitting with him, he shook his head in disbelief and ran for help. To his rescue came a black porter. The two of them escorted us to the Jim Crow car. I think Dad did such things to be ornery. We all had a good laugh talking about the shocked, distressed looks everyone had when we came and sat with Dad.

Since Dad was a railroad employee, we could ride the train free . . . a great advantage even though we had to sit in the Jim Crow cars with their shabby, unpadded seats. It would always be one of the older cars with no bathroom facilities and no modern heating stoves, just tiny little potbellied stoves. The regular cars had finely polished wood and brass and were equipped with heaters for the winter, ice-water dispensers for the summer, and commodes that were serviced at each stop. But we had other advantages. In Mother's enormous hatbox, we carried fried chicken and bread and butter that were the best you could find anywhere. We kids liked the Jim Crow car because it was just one car away from the engine with only the fireman's open car in-between. So we could see what went on in the two most important areas of the train's operation. What fun it was to sit on the side seats right by the open window and watch the engineer pull the train whistle. I was in awe of the fireman's muscles as he shoveled coal into the boiler. But I think I was most impressed by the engineer because I knew he had to be pretty smart to be responsible for the safety of all those people riding the train.

W.G.

Almost all our friends, including kids, called Dad "W.G." My mom and sisters called him "Daddy," while my brothers and I used "Pop." White folks generally called him "Bill." He loved

children and attracted them to him, but he was strict and expected them to behave. There wasn't any generation gap in those
days—he closed it with a razor strap. But he rarely used it. He
didn't need it most of the time. We all knew what was expected
of us and were happy to oblige. We had a sense of purpose and
necessity about the work we did because W.G. didn't treat us like
kids. He was interested in what we did and helped us learn better
ways of doing things. He'd be real patient and say, "Try holding
the hammer this way—it'll work better" or "Use the ax like this."

All the boys helped stack firewood for the heating stoves, the
clothes-washing stove, and Momma's cookstove. After supper every night, Dad would have us four boys take turns on the two-man
saw until each one of us was worn out. Even though he'd done a
full day's work, he could outlast us all in cutting wood. Since we
had no washing machine, Mom would scrub on a washboard,
sometimes until her hands bled.

I remember one time Dad was digging a well by hand. He
wouldn't use a ladder; he just put his feet across the width of the
hole and worked his way up and down slowly. I can still taste that
clear, clean, cold water.

He worked evenings as a deputy sheriff during part of the time
we lived in Collinsville. I suppose he got the job initially because
of his looks: he was white, husky, and dignified. You could see
he was someone to be reckoned with. But he kept the job because
of his skill and personality. He didn't even carry a gun, but since
he was a pretty good prizefighter, he really didn't need one. When
he had to take someone in, they'd usually just say, "Okay, Bill."
Besides, there was a general respect for the law in those days.

He was some man. I used to marvel at how those big hands of
his were so quick and skillful playing the piano or guitar. He
never had a lesson on either, but he was good. He wasn't a singer
but would talk his way through the lyrics in such a way it would
bring tears to your eyes. We'd sing along on the songs we knew.
He'd play for hours, shifting from Scott Joplin to the old standards like "Darktown Strutters' Ball" and "Carry Me Back to
Old Virginny." Sometimes he'd bring home the latest tune he'd
learned while he was a bouncer at the local theater. Dad played
a gourd mandolin from Italy that he had purchased, and he

taught Mom to play guitar. She'd play the melody—what he called obligato. They'd play for us in the evenings while we'd drink lemonade. Sometimes Dad would do the buck-and-wing, a tap dance that I think is a combination of an Irish clog and African jig. It seemed like making music together was a tremendous bond for Dad and Mom, and it was a real model for how a good marriage should be.

We had a Victrola with a big horn on it and a picture of Nipper, a terrier dog, with a patch of white around one eye. We had lots of different kinds of records, but Mom especially loved Amelita Galli-Curci, the famous Italian soprano, and the great Caruso.

It's not surprising we all showed an interest in music as we grew older. Edith played the piano and was the only one of us to take singing lessons. I bought a bass in my teens and just started playing. We all liked to dance; my sisters and I won many contests for ballroom dancing.

Fishing with W.G.

W.G. was a determined man, too. One time when he was fishing in Omaha, he had a particularly large, feisty carp on the line. He worked and worked trying to land it, until finally the fishing line broke and the fish swam away. But Dad just jumped right in after it . . . and, by golly, he caught it. When he came out of the water, W.G. had his hand in the gill of this four-foot-long fish with a huge belly. With one that big, you really had to know what you were doing. The back fin could cut you like a knife. The fish still had the hook in it and a piece of the line. He said, "Get the washtub and move it over here." I wasn't crazy about the idea, but I sure didn't want to be responsible for losing the fish, so I dragged the tub over very carefully.

We ate fish for nearly a month, and to this day I avoid fish when possible. We ate fried fish, baked fish, fish patties, fish sandwiches, cured fish, and fish salad. Mom smoked or salted some of it, but mostly she kept it in the icebox, getting new ice every other day.

Mom

Mom was a wonder, too. She was dark brown and had a very proud bearing. She'd walk so regally that people seemed to enjoy just watching her go by. She could do so many things so well. She was a good seamstress, so she always dressed well. She could take a man's suit and remake it into a woman's suit. She took drapes that people gave her and made them into beautiful evening gowns. When they saw what she could do with their cast-offs, they'd hire her to sew for them.

She recited poetry beautifully and so was constantly called on by the church groups for recitations. One I remember most clearly is "The Curfew Shall Not Ring Tonight" about Oliver Cromwell. He was to die when the curfew bell rang. The woman who loved him climbed the tower and held onto the bell to keep it from ringing. That picture was so clear in my mind and still is today. I could just see her clinging to the bell with hands bleeding to save the man she loved.

Mom had gone to a black college in Normal, Illinois, now the home of Illinois State University. She got a teaching certificate there and was teaching in Collinsville when she met Dad. I don't remember their ever talking about their romance, but she must have been quite a catch. She was beautiful, educated, and an outstanding dancer and reciter.

Dad was five years older than Mom, but he lived until his eighties while she died in her sixties. They were very devoted to one another. Dad never left the house without kissing her good-bye and then would kiss her when he returned. She would always save special food treats for Dad, and he would occasionally bring her something from town. Her favorite was smoked salmon. He'd buy a big package, and she'd eat it a little at a time, all by herself.

In the evenings Mom would recite poetry for us at home and give us reading assignments even before I was old enough to go to school. We read the Bible and took turns giving the prayer at dinner. When it was your turn, you'd better be prepared. I still miss the family dinners in the kitchen around the big table. My wife, Evelyn, and I continued that tradition with our children, but now that is gone, too.

I can remember seeing Mom working with the older children while we lived in Collinsville. She was always busy cooking, cleaning, and caring for us. But my most dramatic memory is of her doing the cakewalk, a dance step blacks invented where you rear back and take big steps across the room. The "walk" is similar to the strut that majorettes use when they lead marching bands. The famous dance teams Williams and Walker and Broomfield and Greeley made the "walk" popular. Also, Mom was an excellent ballroom dancer and cut quite a figure dancing in the fancy dresses and gowns she made.

Collinsville and Characters

I was of preschool age the whole time I lived in Collinsville, so most of my memories center around my home and family. We didn't go into town much, mostly because there was nothing there for us. There were no black-owned businesses, and blacks weren't allowed to try on clothes in the stores. Besides, Mom made a lot of our clothes, and we bought the others at the Salvation Army store. Everything was cheaper there. They also sold groceries and hardware items. There were no black doctors or dentists, but there was a Jewish doctor, Dr. Martin Schrippel, who took care of blacks and even made house calls.

There were some real characters in our part of Collinsville, one we used to chant about. We'd say, "Down in the holler—see old man Gregor." His name was really Gregory. He'd kind of growl and say, "Hello there, I'm the baddest nigger here," so apparently "bad" has been "good" for a long time. He was so big and rough-talking he was scary to me.

He drove the scavenger wagon, picking up cast-offs and reselling them for his livelihood. He also collected garbage and sold it for hog feed. I'll never forget how he'd stand in his backyard in the morning and yell "Hey!" The pigs and chickens would come running like they were his children.

Another character was Easy Ware, a real fine lightweight boxer. He dressed so well he was called a "real dude." Pete Shaffer wore spats and gambler-striped pants. He probably was a gambler or maybe a hustler. You had to wonder because he lived like a well-to-do person, a rich white man, but didn't seem to do much. His house had a brick fireplace with beautiful rugs and furniture.

Because of the hills in town, we had a split-level house, long before architects designed houses that way. For a while, we rented one level to a woman who had a friend named Parker. I surmised he was her boyfriend. She'd get all dressed up in a long green skirt and different kinds of blouses. I thought she looked real good. Then she'd make coffee and yell out "Porker," her way of pronouncing his name. He'd come and have coffee, and they'd talk and laugh.

Moving Experience

During these next few years, we moved three times, but it really didn't bother me. At that age, home was wherever my family was.

World War I was under way, and although Dad was of draft age, he had too many dependents for the military. However, he had job skills needed in the war effort, and, under the Manpower Mobility Act, he was drafted to work at the Rock Island Arsenal, on an island in the Mississippi River between Rock Island and Davenport, as a millwright making rifle butts.

To get to Davenport, we went by train through St. Louis where we had quite a wait. I was four and had an experience that still haunts me today. I remember walking to the edge of the Washington St. bridge and looking over the railing to the riverfront below. I saw what I thought were cattle pens. A white policeman was passing by, and I didn't know I wasn't supposed to talk to him. I asked what the pens were for, and he said they were slave pens. Then Dad explained it to me, and that is my first memory of knowing about slavery. I didn't fully understand what he told me, but I felt a strong, sickening fear sweep over me—a feeling I still feel even now when I think of those pens.

Davenport was and *felt* segregated even though it had much more to offer blacks than Collinsville. There were a few black-owned restaurants and a black barbershop, and blacks could attend the white Catholic church. My Aunt Ollie's husband had a shoeshine parlor and ran the city scavenger wagons and the drays that took people to and from the train depot. In spite of all this, I heard grown-ups say that whites didn't like to see blacks downtown. But we had lots of family around, and that's what mattered to me. Grandma Lee, my mother's mother, lived with us part of the time, and there were aunts, uncles, and cousins in town.

Even though I was young, I remember hearing about the war. People worried about it all the time, especially my Aunt Ollie, my mother's sister, who had two sons in the army. But what a day when they came marching home! We stayed at Aunt Ollie's when we first moved to Davenport, so I saw it all from her house. As they marched up Harrison Street and saw their mother, they broke rank and ran over to hug her. I had burned the bottoms of my feet the previous week on the old potbellied stove, so I couldn't go outside. But I watched this drama unfold by scrambling and crawling from one window to another.

Alfie Black was one of these returning heroes. He was in a company that had participated in a battle that won him a French medal. He'd say, "When we got through shooting, we had cleaned them out. There was nothing left but stumps smoking."

Other memories of those times in Davenport are mainly about airplanes. I would lie on the grass and watch those planes with single and double wings. When I'd see three stacked wings, I'd really get excited. Only a few of them had the latest swept wings.

The great flu epidemic was another worry in those days. Many people died from it. We had some neighbors called the Manions who had several husky sons. They were nearly professional-level boxers and wrestlers. They came down with the flu, and Grandma helped cure them with pig-toe tea. It was nasty-tasting stuff that looked like pond scum, but the Manions were sure it had saved them. Out of gratitude from then on, the Manion boys would come to our defense when there'd be trouble with neighborhood kids.

When the war ended, Dad wasn't needed at the arsenal anymore. They were hiring at the meat-packing plant in Omaha, so once again we moved. By this time I was seven or eight and beginning to be more interested in the world outside my family.

Polish Neighbors

Omaha was no melting pot. But in our area, there was an un-segregated mixture of blacks and whites (mostly Polish). Today you might say that our neighborhood was "in transition." It had been built thirty years earlier by whites who worked in the pack-inghouses. They were thrifty folks who saved their money, started businesses of their own, then moved on to better areas. It was a natural, ongoing process. European immigrants and blacks re-placed them in their houses, jobs, and neighborhood businesses.

It seemed like each ethnic group favored certain kinds of busi-nesses: the Polish and Czechoslovakians would have dry goods and grocery stores, bakeries, bars, and butcher shops. The Greeks specialized in restaurants, fruit markets, and grocery stores. There must have been a few Lebanese and Syrian people in the area, because I remember the beautiful baskets of imported dried fruits in their grocery stores. When there were enough blacks in a neighborhood to warrant starting businesses, they seemed to favor such operations as shoeshine parlors, cleaning and press-ing, food service, and barbershops. The barbershops were usually located in adjacent neighborhoods because they were for whites only. It's ironic that these black owners could not get their hair cut in their own shops!

Having a residential area next to a packinghouse wasn't a prob-lem for any of the ethnic groups who lived there. It made sense to live close to your work since working people in those days didn't own cars. We were one of a few black families, so we rarely ventured out of the immediate area.

The women all wore long skirts and hats, even in the hottest days of summer. It must have been difficult for them to stay so clean-looking—but they always were. We used to marvel at the Polish women who worked in the packinghouse. They'd move heavy stacks of meat from place to place on two-wheeled carts so the men could do the cutting. Then, just like most women today, they did the cooking and cleaning after work. But the Polish men were busy and hardworking, too. They'd help each other build barns and outhouses or put in sidewalks.

Blacks were laborers, meatpackers, and butchers at the plant. They worked comfortably with whites, but there was little mixing socially. It was the same for blacks in other work situations. Some unions (or guilds as they were often called) would accept you as a member but not as a social partner. Many unions did not accept blacks, and so most joined the coal miners' union. This union already had many blacks in it, probably because our black forefathers worked in mines in Africa and brought their skills with them. It didn't matter which union you belonged to, as long as you had a card. They respected you for what you could do. Perhaps this is one reason why work is so important to me; getting respect for your skills and effort was a powerful incentive.

Socializing with our Polish neighbors was not a problem for the children, at least young children. We all had a ball together throughout childhood until the teen years, and then it stopped. This was just one of the taboos we grew up with. We learned to be quiet and polite in all dealings with grown-ups. Dad said to be gentlemen and ladies. This was the norm throughout the area, for black and white.

Real Cowboys

We had real cowboys in those days, and they'd come driving cattle through town to the packinghouse at the south end of Omaha. Most of the blacks lived in the vicinity of 24th and Q streets, which was dusty, dirt-packed, and lined with small wooden houses and a few stores. It was a narrow street that usually bustled with children, dogs, horses and wagons, and an occasional noisy automobile.

Since this area was on the way to the packinghouse, the ranchers just drove their cattle right down the middle of 24th Street. It sounded like an army marching, but we didn't mind. It was exciting to the kids and profitable for the grown-ups. All the houses had lean-to porches on the front of them. When the cattle came thundering down the streets, the steers' horns would knock down the posts that held up the porches. To make amends, the trail boss would follow along and pay each owner $5 or $10 to replace the posts. Dad made the most of the situation! He reinforced the supports for the roof, and then he'd just lean the porch posts up against the roof. So they *always* fell down, and he *always* collected money from the trail boss, with no harm done to our porch.

Dad and Mom would talk to the cowboys, but the kids were shooed into the house when the cattle came. We each had a special vantage point for watching the goings-on. The noise was tremendous, but we were too fascinated to miss anything.

The cowboys weren't much like you saw in the early movies. They were all sizes and shapes—and colors. Some were black, some white, some Mexicans, and some Indians. Their faces were unshaven and dirty, their clothing tattered and grimy. In the winter, they wore large red or blue hankies across their noses and mouths to protect them from the bitter cold air. Most of them wore sheepskin coats with the wool on the inside. The coats had a canvas covering which made the men look like skinned sheep. The horses looked strange, too. They were especially scary in winter; because of the frigid air, their mouths were ringed by frost, and they snorted streams of white frost. To our young eyes they were fearsome, like the steeds of the Four Horsemen of the Apocalypse that Mom had told us about. Other times when they exhaled, we thought they looked like steam engines.

These cowboys didn't wear proud white hats like the Lone Ranger's; they were flat-brimmed, sweat-stained leather ones, all misshapen and droopy. And *these* cowboys carried no guns. But were *we* impressed! We used to listen intently from our peepholes to hear the exchanges between the grown-ups. Sometimes the folks would come in with a juicy bit of information, but most of their conversations were about the weather, a matter of great interest to the cowboys. The winter cold and summer sandstorms could peel the skin off your forehead if you weren't protected. When I got older, I realized that this must have been the beginning of the dust bowl.

I was really impressed by these working cowboys. Later, I was even more impressed by the razzle-dazzle of show cowboys who used to travel around the country with Annie Oakley, putting on rodeos in small towns. One was Bill Pickett, the first black cowboy in the Cowboy Hall of Fame. He got there because he was the first man to bulldog a steer—and he did it when the rodeo came to Estherville, Iowa. Yes, he was special, but two men who traveled with the show also turned out to be pretty important: Will Rogers, an Indian cowboy who became a well-known philosopher and humorist, and Tom Mix, a Mexican American who was the first great cowboy film star of Spanish heritage. But the biggest thrill for me was Annie Oakley herself, performing her famous feats such as shooting light bulbs as they were thrown in the air. She had beautiful western-style clothes. I'd never seen such long blond hair, and she was riding in a fine-looking touring car with the top down.

Haunted House

Although I didn't know who he was at the time, it was during this period that I met Father Flanagan, the famous Catholic priest who founded Boys Town. He had a run-down old house next door to the 24th Street firehouse in Omaha where my friends and I hung around. We used to love to watch the horse-drawn fire engines rush by. With their ears laid back, the horses would charge out of the firehouse, pulling the pump truck. They were beautifully groomed with immaculate white coats, pink noses, and shiny hooves. Part of our fun, too, was fantasizing about Father Flanagan's house, which was the first site of what later became Boys Town. We believed it was haunted and used to imagine strange sounds and activities. One day this priest came by and asked us to pass out bills expounding Father Flanagan's message: "There's no such thing as a bad boy." He gave us five cents for our trouble. Actually, it was no trouble—the thought of having anything to do with a haunted house was enough excitement to keep us chattering for a week.

When Father Flanagan started Boys Town it was called a "home for wayward boys." Now they say it is for "neglected" boys; to me, wayward boys often have been neglected. Boys Town has evolved into a huge home and school for boys and girls. It's currently located on a beautiful acreage at the edge of Omaha.

These, my earliest memories, are almost totally of comfortable, easy times. I'm sure Mom and Dad knew about lots of frightening things going on because the Ku Klux Klan was very active. But they kept most of that talk away from us and protected us from those kinds of worries as much as they could. We grew up thinking that our way of life was the norm for blacks. But our next move, to Estherville, Iowa, opened a window on the black world outside the small rural towns of the Midwest. We didn't go to that world in person but learned about it second- and third-hand from the many railworkers who came to visit us in our Estherville boxcar home.

3   **B**oxcars and Schooldays

When Dad went to work for the arsenal during World War I, the Rock Island Railroad promised him his job back when the emergency was over. They were as good as their word; after the war, the railroad sent him to the Sioux Falls division in Estherville, a small white town in the northwest part of Iowa. This move posed a problem for the railroad because there was no place for black families to live.

The railroad owned quite a bit of property, so they set some aside for our family to live on. It was located at the edge of town—acres and acres of rolling green land with trees and a river. They brought two boxcars out to us and put them parallel, leaving a space between them. Then Dad connected them by building a large room in the space. He finished off this middle part of the house with a large sitting room, dining room, and two bedrooms. He made the boxcar on the front of the house into a huge kitchen with eating space. We always ate there (except on Sundays) and would spend most of our evenings there. It was similar to today's family room. The boxcar on the back of the house had two more bedrooms. We had an outdoor toilet, and our indoor plumbing consisted of a pitcher pump in the kitchen. Dad put the well in himself along with a large pump outside.

Dad built a nice porch on the side where the front room was. He put up latticework and planters so Mom could grow flowers. He left up the ladders that the boxcar came with. We kids would climb up them and pretend we were brakemen and engineers on a real train. Since our boxcar house was made from refrigerator cars, it was well insulated, so it was warm in the winter and cool in the summer.

Years later during the housing shortage that developed after the end of World War II, we saw some homes on the southwest side of Cedar Rapids that looked just like our boxcar home. Apparently, someone had decided to use the Rock Island's strategy for housing the Reed family to solve a postwar problem.

Mom grew flowers all over the place, and we had a large garden. We kids did the weeding for both the flower and vegetable gardens. Dad made sure that the rows were straight and that we kept the gardens very clean. Mother canned for winter from the garden, so we always had plenty of vegetables to eat. It wasn't always so with meat; I was surprised when I started working in restaurants and learned that one person would eat a whole steak. At home, we all shared one steak when we were lucky enough to have it. And many meals were all vegetables. I guess that was good for us though, since nutritionists today are telling us to cut back on the amount of meat we eat.

Neighbors

Our boxcar home was located at the farthest edge of Estherville. Many of the local people were of Swedish descent. I remember one person in particular—a big strong kid named Takias who
always took up for us when there was trouble with other children.

Mrs. Ketchum lived farther away in one of those precut houses
from the Sears catalog. They put part of it up in the fall, stacked
lumber all around the foundation, and covered the rest with canvas. That winter when it got icy, we slid from the top of the canvas
to the bottom. In the spring the rest of the house went up almost
overnight. The idea of a precut house kit was a true innovation in
housing, and one that worked. The house is still standing today.
In later years, I have seen ads in papers and magazines about
precut houses as if they were something new.

Our house was at the end of the town's main drag, which was
all of eight blocks long. To me, the most important businesses
were the Englert Theater and the drugstore. The older kids took
us to the silent movies and for Cokes and candy at the drugstore.
There was never any trouble going there, I suppose because there
weren't many of us and we were well behaved.

Since our place was at the very edge of town yet only three
blocks from its center, you can see that Estherville wasn't much
of a town in terms of its size. Even so, it was forward-looking
enough to have a junior college—a rarity in those days. Estherville Junior College had integrated track meets and attracted a
number of activities to town, including lecturers and concerts.

There was a certain amount of hazing at school which we
learned to deal with, each of us in different ways. Probably the
worst problem we suffered was the isolation. There were no black
merchants, no black doctors or dentists, no activities we could
attend with comfort. There were four black families in the Estherville area, not counting ours. In these families, there were
seventeen children. The Nances and Robinsons were farmers who
lived at the edge of town. The other two black families were our
relatives. Bessie Blake, my mother's niece, and her husband,
Leon Blake, lived near us and continued to live in Estherville
until just recently. Leon was a welder at the Rock Island round-

house. Bessie was not typical of homemakers in those days; she was an outstanding speaker who spoke all over the country for the white Methodist Church. The other relatives were Aunt Altheta and Uncle Al Moore. Aunt Theta, as we called her, was a very successful realtor who later did very well with a big housing development in Kansas City. Uncle Al was a cook on the dining car for the railroad. I think he may have been Puerto Rican. He had straight black hair and wasn't very dark. He had a peg leg but could run like the dickens.

There was a black couple, the McCwillas, who lived in Estherville, too. Mrs. McCwilla talked kind of fast and ran her words together. One time she sent me to the store for a can of okra. Well, I'd never heard of okra, so I came back with a can opener. Mr. McCwilla was the janitor at the train depot and had real painful rheumatism. Midol was the only medicine that would help. When someone told him it was a medicine for "female troubles" he didn't seem to care. He said, "It kind of salivates me, but it makes the pain go away." The last time I talked to him, he was still using it.

Aunt Theta and Uncle Al had six children: Beatrice, Lillian, Albert, Gage, Booker, and Ethelbert. Gage became a doctor but contracted hepatitis when he was in the army and died young. Ethelbert became a singer, but not in the style of his near-namesake, Engelbert Humperdinck, the Englishman who wows them at Las Vegas. It's odd that Engelbert is so popular in the United States while Ethelbert achieved his greatest success in England. Booker became a deputy sheriff in Kansas City, Missouri; Al studied animal husbandry at Tuskegee; Lillian married a doctor and lived in Des Moines until her death in 1991; and Beatrice died several years ago in Los Angeles. None of them are alive today. These cousins who were my playmates and closest friends for so many years scattered all over the country, and so I rarely saw them. But I still have warm memories of the good times we had together.

Visits from relatives who lived elsewhere were rare back then. One visitor was Uncle George, my dad's brother. He traveled around the world on steamships as a porter or stoker in the boiler room. He would work long enough to get a stake for gambling, his true vocation. I guess he was pretty successful at gambling; he always had fancy clothes and presents for us. When I was grown and saw *Death of a Salesman*, the uncle in that play reminded me of Uncle George. He would tell us stories about other countries where he was accepted socially and could go to the best hotels and nightclubs. He had real Indian hair—black and straight. I've lost track of him but did hear that he got married in Chicago and had two sons who both became lawyers.

The Disappearing Dog

We always had a cat and dog. One was a collie named Jack. Uncle Leon also had a dog named Jack, but it was an Airedale. One time, the older boys took Jack the Airedale swimming, and he disappeared in quicksand. They went home in despair. To their great shock, he suddenly appeared before them. The grownups said that he had probably gotten caught in a "floater" (a sandbar), sunk through the bar, got to the water below, and swam out. This is a perfectly reasonable explanation, but it was such a shock to have Jack reappear. I think all the kids still believed it was something magical.

By this time I was of school age. I walked about two miles with my sisters and brother to the area where four Estherville schools were clustered: the elementary, junior high, and high school and Estherville Junior College.

Picture Window

Even though Estherville was remote and we were pretty isolated there, I realize now that we had a big picture window to the rest of the country. Estherville was on the Sioux Falls division of the Rock Island Railroad and had many black employees—mostly brakemen, chefs, and porters—with layovers there. Since they weren't allowed to stay in the hotels in town, the railroad put in dormitories near the depot. These black workers were constant visitors at our house. Brakemen and porters would come by in the summer for picnics. And in the winter, Mom would cook up meals or the chefs would cook for us. They were good cooks and better storytellers. We'd be spellbound for hours listening to their stories about the outside world. That's how we knew what was happening to other blacks across the country. This was true networking before the term was ever used. We heard about lynchings and cross burnings, strikes and race riots. We also heard about the latest songs and dances, fads and fun that blacks were enjoying in other parts of the country. And we learned about the railroad jobs available to blacks, one of the few employment areas where you could make decent money. They were all in service areas: cooks, waiters, Pullman porters. Black college students wanted to be porters when they graduated because money was good and the job prestigious in the black community.

Black railroad employees had their own kind of caste system. There were the gandy dancers who laid track and cleaned out grass from between the ties. "Gandy dancer" was considered a derogatory term then, but we admired them. Their work was hard—carrying ties, pounding the big spikes, bending and lifting in the hot sun. They took pride in keeping the gravel around the ties looking clean. They lived in bunk beds of special cars. They got water for cooking, washing, and drinking from the railroad water towers. To us kids, the most interesting thing about them was the two-man carts they used to move track. It looked like so much fun going twenty miles an hour down the track. Actually, it was hard. It took a lot of energy to pump the handle up and down. Their inspector, the district superintendent, would always be a white man who rode around on the tracks in a small car with railroad wheels on it. This vehicle fascinated us, too. We never got to ride in either kind. The gandys were almost entirely blacks and Mexicans. For the few whites who were gandys, it was a job of last resort, although the benefits and pay were good. It was just very hard work and had a low status in the eyes of some folks.

Pullman porters, on the other hand, had high status. They were especially proud and modeled their speech and manners after whites. Porters also saw an unattractive side of white travelers. They told about men and women meeting their secret lovers on trips or traveling with someone other than their spouse. Because porters were acquainted with the families after a few trips, they knew who belonged with whom. Needless to say, they got big tips.

But it wasn't only fear of having a secret revealed that earned tips; the porters would call white passengers by name, compliment them, brush off their clothes, and just generally make them feel important.

The railroad workers kept us updated on other things, too. For instance, they told us about automobiles and machinery that we had little access to on our Iowa island.

Fancy Food

One fellow I remember in particular was called Tassan, a Puerto Rican. He was a dining-car cook, the one in charge. He was a mixture of black and Spanish. He was light with straight hair and was a Catholic.

As you remember, I wasn't fond of fish, but the baked fish he served us was something else. He brought his knives all rolled in linen when he came to cook for us. He'd bring meat and bread and fancy sauces with him. It was a real show to watch as he filleted the fish, then added tomatoes and spices with a flair! He made carp taste better than trout.

Those dinners were almost magical. We ate in the dining room with its elegant cherry furniture. The table was set with our best glassware and fine linens. We'd polish the silverware with ashes and water.

The grown-ups sat around and talked afterward. The kids ate in the kitchen, but we hung around in the doorways and listened. They might have added to their stories because they were rather competitive storytellers. Occasionally they'd whisper some parts and burst into laughter. We didn't understand everything we heard even when it was loud enough to hear.

The brakemen and porters would be out on their runs for a week at a time, so it was lonely for them. Our family was isolated from other blacks, so we were a source of comfort to each other. We helped them feel they had family around, and our family felt less isolated. If they got sick, there was always a doctor on the company rolls—although it was a white doctor. Most of the time they took care of themselves unless it was something really serious. Blacks didn't go to town unless it was absolutely necessary, nor did they make other kinds of contacts with whites.

Black Success Stories

Waiters and porters would tell how blacks were making it big in white theaters. We heard about the large cities before we ever saw them. They told of black success stories such as Madam C. J. Walker, who made hair preparations and cosmetics for blacks. She became a millionaire.

These railroad workers talked about the great black sports figures of the time such as Jack Johnson, the heavyweight champion, and Sam Langford, a light heavyweight. Blacks were beginning to be a real factor in boxing. While it was a brutal business, the ring was one place you could make a lot of money in a short time and achieve fame overnight.

We learned, too, about the man who owned the *Chicago Defender*, a black newspaper. They'd bring us copies of it. We loved seeing pictures of black professionals. It let us know blacks could make it. We read about Howard University, the prestigious black university where the richest African blacks sent their children for training in such fields as engineering and medicine. Of course, we got some of these success stories from the *Iowa Bystander*, a black newspaper started by Bradley J. Morris. It's still going today, and it still reports statewide news of interest to blacks. Knowing about successful blacks built pride and helped us have higher expectations for ourselves.

On to Cedar Rapids

Dad got an opportunity to be a custodian at Union Station in Cedar Rapids. He could work for both the Rock Island and the Northwestern railroads and get double paychecks. I think, too, he thought it would be good for us to be in a larger town with more blacks. So in 1923 when I was ten, we moved to Cedar Rapids.

The town had a lot to offer, which we often didn't understand or appreciate until sometime later. My sisters and brother went to

McKinley High where their art teacher was named Grant Wood, the same artist who later produced the famous painting *American Gothic*.

The neighborhoods were quite a mixture of economic levels: white middle- and upper-class families were neighborly with us but didn't actually socialize. They'd be there if someone died or was ill, but there was no mixing per se. Then there were the black entrepreneurs who were usually a little bit better off than other blacks. There was Dad Baker's restaurant, pool hall, and barbershop in downtown Cedar Rapids. Nearby was Mr. Nelson's billiard hall and barbershop. On the main street was Mr. Ragland's tailor shop and cleaning/pressing service. Just around the corner were Earl Toom's large shoeshine parlor and Billy and Roy's fast-food restaurant. Mr. Smith at the white Elks Club managed the whole place and kept it running properly. This was the first time I'd seen blacks running anything.

There was a great deal of Ku Klux Klan activity in the country during those postwar times, probably because blacks who'd served in the military and worked in factories were not content to go back to the lives they'd had before the war. However, Cedar Rapids did not have a problem, at least as far as the whites were concerned. There were so few of us, I suppose we posed no threat. The same situation was true in many other towns in the county. One or two families per town did not seem to bother whites. While we heard of lynchings and cross burnings in the more populated areas of the country, we felt no sense of danger.

It's ironic that the worst discrimination I heard about was against people of German descent. During the war and afterward, they were suspected of being disloyal to the United States. They were called "Gerries" and "Krauts" and were run out of many small towns. In fact, someone blew up the house of a doctor of German descent who lived a block away from us.

Color Matters

That first fall when I started school at Adams Elementary was a confusing, hurtful time for me. I had played with the white children who lived near our house, and we'd had a fine time. But at school those same playmates would call me names or just simply ignore me. At first I was puzzled and hurt. I soon realized that they were embarrassed or afraid to be my friend in front of other whites. I never jeopardized them by revealing that we were playmates. Even today, I tell my white friends I won't compromise our friendship by trying to socialize with them around their friends who may not feel as they do. Although I have been criticized by other blacks for this, I feel it is sensible and accomplishes more in the long run than confrontation. My folks taught us not to fight or carry hard feelings when these things happened. Mama told us we'd just have to pray that these people would learn better. We were strong, healthy kids who could have held our own in a fight, but Dad said that the test of a man is in knowing he can whip another person physically but choosing not to.

There were no black teachers at Adams, but the white teachers did not seem prejudiced. In fact, when they'd see we were having a tough time, they'd try to give us special attention and favors. Once when they were inspecting all the children's hair for lice, Miss Adams, the school principal, just waved us on through the line saying, "Their mother keeps their hair too clean to get lice."

In spite of all that my teachers and parents said and did, some of the things that happened still hurt a lot. When a fight occurred between kids of different races, you heard "fight—fight—nigger and the white." And it was just normal for every black man to be called "George" if not "nigger." And black women were automatically called by their first names. Whites seemed to be unaware that this might be painful or insulting. White grown-ups would call little black kids names such as "chocolate drop" or "snowball," probably not realizing that even "cute" names hurt. But I learned behaviors that helped me survive many threatening and humiliating experiences. I learned how and when to fight. You had to be prepared to fight more than one person in a fight with whites. They'd gang up on you at times, so you avoided situations when you might be considerably outnumbered.

It was sometimes helpful to challenge the worst kid in the

town—as long as you could whip him. Then the others would leave you alone. And sometimes he'd just back down. It was a chance you didn't take unless a situation had been building and was intolerable, for instance, being picked on every night on the way home from school until you were virtually forced to defend yourself. Then I would make short work of the toughest guy in the group before a crowd gathered. You could fight while you were still young and not get into trouble, but when you got older, you'd get a bad reputation or get arrested.

It was during this time that I developed a tension, a state of alertness in the company of whites, that I am rarely without even today. While I hardly ever experience a threatening or even embarrassing situation today, my body automatically assumes a state of self-defense. I think today it is called the "fight or flight" syndrome. In those days, it was a necessary defense mechanism; without it, I might not have made it through the next years of my life, as I left the protection of home and made my way through school.

White Role Models

But then there'd be the one white person who'd offer to help you. Someone who'd show you a kindness or give you a hand. I remember the town blacksmith, George Niery, who made me a ring out of horseshoe nails. It looked neat, and if I ever got into a fight, the square nailhead could really cut a guy up. But George had nothing like that in mind. He was a big burly man with a gruff voice but very kind. Regularly, he took me to his church and then to eat at the cafeteria afterward. I couldn't have gone to either of those places on my own.

When George passed on, an insurance man named Anderson took me under his wing, and we went to his church, the First Presbyterian. Sadly, when the crash came in the thirties, Mr. Anderson jumped out of a big bank building and killed himself.

Many other whites in Cedar Rapids opened doors for me. Police Chief Benesh, Bob Vlach, Bob Caldwell, Bud Jensen, and Howard Hall were my role models then, throughout my teen years, and, I guess, for life. They might have seemed to be just ordinary people, but to me they were very important.

The Iceman Cometh

Another white man we kids admired a great deal was the Hubbard Ice Company man. He was tall, muscled, and polite. He always had a plug of tobacco in his mouth. He wore a thick black rubber tunic to keep his clothes dry. He'd carry a hundred pounds of ice up to our place and chip off twenty-five-pound pieces. Combined with his dangerous-looking ice tongs, he was an awesome sight to little kids. He was kind of a showoff, too: he'd lift a fifty-pound square of ice on each shoulder without any trouble. He called us kids "Mr." and "Mrs." and gave us chips of ice. We followed him and his wagon around whenever he was in the neighborhood. He had a big scale on his wagon to weigh the ice. Hubbard's got ice from the Cedar River. They'd cut it out with a big saw machine, put it on runners that led to a very large storage barn, then they'd store it in straw. It was amazing how it kept all summer. At ice-cutting time, the fishermen would gather around because the fish would come up for air and take bait while they were there. So everyone profited—but the fish!

Black Professionals

Our one black professional in Cedar Rapids was a dentist named Hutchensen (Hutch) Burshears. He started the first black Boy Scout troop (#12) in Iowa. He rented the Odd Fellows hall once a week. We'd go there to box, work on our merit badges, work out, and shoot baskets, and we'd finish up with a bottle of pop. More important, he taught us about good sportsmanship and helped us build self-esteem. He'd invite our folks in for ceremonies when we'd get our badges. It was great to be a part of something big.

Dr. Burshears talked to several Scout executives and arranged for us to go to a Boy Scout camp at the same time white troops were there. Getting ready to go was really exciting for us. We'd never been to camp before. Moms pressed our uniforms and advised us about clean underwear. I almost got a complex thinking that if I ever did get in an accident, the doctors would say, "There's that Reed kid, check his drawers to see if they're clean."

Three or four black men with nice cars volunteered to take us to camp. Two of them were chauffeurs and had limo-type automobiles. We were to leave at 8 A.M. Monday, and it was awfully hard to sleep Sunday night. By 6 A.M. I was on the front porch with all my gear, anxiously waiting for my ride to come by. In those days we had touring cars, and it was fun driving with the top down. The camp was near Stone City, about twenty-five miles north and east of Cedar Rapids. It seemed like it took forever, but finally we arrived at Green Mansion, a property donated to the Scouts by a man who had owned a stone quarry. It was called Camp Mishawaka.

Our counselors were a bunch of Coe College athletes who worked at the camp to make money in the summer. They were white and yet seemed to know no prejudice. Our troop slept in our own tent, but that was true of all the troops. We ate, performed, and played together and enjoyed a lot of activities: horseback riding, starting fires with flintstones, swimming, lifeguard training, volleyball, etc.

One of the tricks the counselors played on us was to take us "snipe hunting." They told us elaborate stories about snipes and how to catch them by beating on the bushes. Of course, snipes don't live in that part of the world, and if they did, you sure couldn't catch them with a gunnysack. But we didn't know that. We were so busy looking for snipes, we didn't notice they'd left us in the woods alone. They stayed nearby but we didn't know it, so we were really scared.

In the troop was a little older and much bigger guy named Beverly Taylor, nicknamed Bev, who became my dear friend for a whole lifetime. Early in the week we were on a hike, and I was feeling weak. I must have been kind of upset by the change of food and maybe a little homesick. Bev stopped and carried me on his back. After that, he sort of took on the role of a big brother to me. We were always close. And even today we're still very good friends.

Burning Cross

We were all having a great time at camp. Then one night we could see a light shining through the tent wall. Someone shouted "fire." We ran to the top of a hill and saw a giant cross burning and people in what looked like hoods. The Scout executives called our counselors out and gave them blank pistols, although I felt that two of them had real pistols. They said, "Now go down there and clean those guys out." The counselors went hurtling down the hill shooting their pistols and chased those guys away. The next morning at breakfast the Scout leader told us, "Troop 12, I want you to volunteer to ride through town on horseback to show those people we're not backing down." So white and black troops rode through town together . . . no doubt to the discomfort of those Klansmen.

This is one of only two times I've ever seen the Ku Klux Klan. The other time was in Iowa City when I was about fifteen. My oldest sister and her husband lived with another couple, Duke and Eta Slater. Duke was one of the greatest All-American tackles at the University of Iowa. He later became a lawyer and then a judge in Chicago, and a residence hall at the university is named in his honor.

Duke and Eta shared an apartment above a billiard hall and worked to help themselves through school. I'd go there in summer to do chores and see what it was like to be with college people. One night they came home early and pulled down all the blinds. I peeked out and saw a giant parade with hooded people carrying signs saying, "Down with Niggers, Catholics, and Jews." The white hoods were of all sizes, so I knew there were children and women there, too.

Coolidge Parade

When Calvin Coolidge was president he came to Cedar Rapids, and the city leaders put on a parade. We lived on Fifth Street, and they held it just two blocks away on Third Street. He came through our neighborhood, which was mostly Czechoslovakian, then went downtown. It was quite a parade. John Phillip Sousa's band led it, and there was a black band from a mining town in southern Iowa called Buxton. Many blacks who "made it" came from there. The procession was led by a very colorful man called Kid Onions who almost did a cakewalk as he directed the parade with two batons.

A few months before the parade, the city brought in black bricklayers to resurface Third Street. That was a show in itself. They didn't just lay brick, it was a performance. They sang and moved with great flair and grace. The street seemed to slowly crawl forward. As they worked in rhythm together, a crowd would gather. The workers all seemed to enjoy performing this beautiful ballet for onlookers.

In those days black workers seemed to make an art of whatever work they did, no matter how menial or rough it was. In the building trades blacks could not achieve journeyman status, i.e., plasterer or brick mason, but they performed the laborious backup services to those jobs. For example, they carried the plaster used to cover inside and outside walls of buildings. They'd climb up ladders with perfect balance without using their hands. It was the same with bricklaying; blacks carried the mortar and bricks to the white masons. They'd balance this wet cement called hod on a mortarboard. Carrying bricks in V-shaped boards required balance and strength. It was a dirty, backbreaking job that they did gracefully. They didn't know that by demonstrating their skillfulness, they were helping blacks get into unions and make other breakthroughs in the trades. Also, the intuitive connection that developed between blacks and whites while they worked with each other must have helped build a sense of trust and respect. Black workers earned respect in other ways as well. White contractors would bring them in for dangerous jobs such as painting water towers and church steeples.

It was during this part of my life that I realized what a difference the color of your skin makes. But even as this dawned upon me, I found that there were many variations in whites' attitudes toward blacks. There were the outright hostile people, those who tolerated us, those who wanted to help us, and those who seemed oblivious to color. As a young boy it was not easy to sort out these subtle differences. But I did have enough white helping hands that I was able to thrive in a white culture. I often compare my experiences with those of the black children growing up in today's inner cities. They have no good black or white role models. They get no rewards for good behavior or for honest work. They have no expectations for learning in school. They have no hope for making an honest living. Living as a fly in the buttermilk was not comfortable, but it enabled me bit by bit to build a method for surviving and eventually thriving. The next years of my life were to be more exciting, more stretching, and more dangerous.

4   In Harm's Way

In 1928 at fifteen years of age I stood 5 feet 9 inches and weighed 175 pounds. I had rapidly grown to be very strong from all the heavy work I did at home and for other people in the community. Riding a bike on my paper route developed my legs, and lawn work was a challenge to all my muscles. Remember, there were no gas-driven lawn mowers, snowblowers, garden tillers, or electric saws in those days.

Although W.G. had taught us boys how to handle ourselves in

a fight, as we reached puberty actually using these skills became too dangerous to consider. Socializing with whites became even less comfortable for them, and we really had to learn to step carefully. I suppose parents worried that romances would develop between the races. Black parents preferred their kids not get involved for the grief it surely held for them. Some claimed to be against it "for the sake of the children" a mixed couple might have. However, this didn't jibe with a saying blacks had: "If you're white you're right, if you're black get back, if you're brown, stick around."

In a way it was a moot point because flies in the buttermilk were so easily seen in small towns it was unthinkable to put yourself in jeopardy by crossing the color line. It would have been certain trouble to even seem interested in a white person of the opposite sex. There were some older mixed couples in town, but they were successful businesspeople. Young people did not risk such situations.

In larger cities it was another matter; there was a lot of mixing and "passing." You could always tell light blacks who were passing themselves off as whites. You might give them a sign that you knew, but you'd never give them away to whites. Even if you weren't passing, being light could lead to some odd situations. I had a friend in a little town north of Cedar Rapids who looked just like a white man. He was married to a very dark, beautiful woman. She had fine features, walnut-colored skin, and a bathing beauty shape. Once a year, Jim and Selma would drive to southern Mississippi to visit her folks. To avoid trouble, he had her ride in the backseat. But getting service at a gasoline station could be a problem, so she'd lie down on the backseat. Many times the white station attendant would wink and smile at Jim when he saw her there. One guy patted him on the shoulder and said, "I see you're going to try changing your luck tonight." Apparently he felt that going to bed with a black woman would bring him good luck! While deep down you always felt angry about this kind of attitude, we'd laugh about "putting something over on them."

It was a given that white men would go to bed with black women but they wouldn't have breakfast with them. In the same way, there have always been clubs, roadhouses, and bootleg joints called black-and-tan spots where whites socialized with blacks. They'd come to *our* territory supposedly for the music. I think they also liked the feeling of doing something kind of risky and rebellious. Then, too, there were those who were truly "soul brothers," or as we used to say in show business, "Man, you in the book." This meant you were such a good musician that you played black music just like a black. Nowadays it means a white dances, cooks, or performs as well as a black.

Time for Work

When you think how dependent teenagers are on their peers and how much energy they spend on socializing, you realize what an impact such limitations might have had upon us. But we didn't dwell on the fact that we couldn't have the kind of social life our white peers had. What we lacked in numbers and opportunity, we made up for in inventiveness. Our groups included younger and older kids, and we attended both Baptist and Methodist youth groups (Baptist Young People's Union and Christian Endeavor). We regularly socialized with blacks in such surrounding towns as Marshalltown, Waterloo, Iowa City, Davenport, and Des Moines. All told, we had a social circle of about three hundred blacks in their teens and twenties.

We'd advertise our dances or parties in newspapers in the college towns, send out fliers, and put ad cards in black stores and businesses. We might rent a dance hall such as the Dreamland, Danceland, or Playmor. In warm weather we'd sometimes rent an outdoor dance pavillion. In Davenport, we'd get the riverboat, the *J. S. Quinlin.* When the whites finished their dances at midnight, ours would begin. Black entertainers who were performing in the area for white functions would often come to our parties afterward. So we'd get to see some of the biggest and best names in show business for free or for very little money. Young and old would come from all over to attend these functions.

In a way, being excluded from high school social activities turned to our advantage. We focused our energies on developing skills that earned money and prepared us to make our way in this

Here I am at seventeen outside old Washington High School in Cedar Rapids, decked out in duds that were cool in those days: a trench coat and a French beret, both of which were purchased at a secondhand store.

world. During these years, I learned how to make most auto and electrical repairs plus skills in building maintenance, cement finishing, cooking, carpentry, and others. These are abilities that helped me all my life, and I wouldn't trade anything for the sense of confidence they gave me.

Truthfully, we spent most of our energies learning to make money. It was the path to survival. The most that black college graduates in those days aspired to was working for the post office or becoming a Pullman porter. While they were admired for their accomplishments and those jobs paid well and were secure, few families could afford to finance even one child through college.

Although education was much admired in our family and by many blacks, schooling often took a backseat to the practicalities of life. Many blacks worked and studied at night to hone their academic skills, some by correspondence and self-study. Luckily, libraries were open to you, and black newspapers carried book lists that would help guide you through learning about various subjects. All of the Reed children graduated from high school, a rarity in those days for black families and even for whites. My alma mater, Washington High School in Cedar Rapids, turned out to have quite a few people who left their mark on the business world: Cherry food-dispenser machines, Nisson trampolines, Lefabureau bookkeeping equipment, and Dieboldt automatic teller machines to name a few. I went to a school reunion in August 1992 and was surprised at how many of us are alive and well.

Newspapers

I started carrying papers for Bill Keeble when I was ten years old and continued until I was fifteen. He bought the papers wholesale and acted as an independent contractor. He was the first white person I ever worked for, and I sure learned a lot from him. I took the job mainly so I could ride a bicycle. We didn't have one at home, and he provided me with a bike. I used to carry three bags of papers at one time: one around my head, one over the handlebars, and one over my shoulders. Mr. Keeble taught me how important it was to be honest and reliable. He always counted the papers out for everyone else, but he came to trust me to fill my own paper bag and wagon. It was a good feeling to know he had faith in my honesty. As a paperboy I also learned the first steps of running my own business. I learned to calculate quickly in my head. Most people were fair with me and would tell me if I made a mistake in their favor.

Mr. Keeble taught me the easy way to multiply: say 59 times

Here I am with television and movie actor Don DeFore at our sixtieth high school reunion for Washington High's class of 1931/32. A good friend, classmate, and neighbor, he is best known for his role as Mr. B on the TV show "Hazel."

12. He said first multiply the 10 times 59 then 2 times 59 and add the two sums, 590 and 118, to get 708, which is much easier than trying to carry in your head. I also got some planning skills from him; I had to figure what it would cost for a wagonload of papers and how much I needed to make from each one to end up with a profit. I continued selling papers, running errands, and

doing household chores into my teens, but as I got older, I became more organized. For example, I realized that selling papers at the Protestant church on Sunday morning only reached one congregation. So I switched to meeting the five Catholic masses at the Immaculate Conception Church. That meant getting up at 4 A.M. on Sundays, riding the bike to Marion about six miles away, then delivering papers to my regular route in time to sell papers at the 6:30 mass and the four that followed.

My high school years were so filled with activities that it's hard now to believe that I did all the things I did. It is also difficult to sort out one from another. In addition to going to school and doing home chores, I would take on any task that made a little money.

Police Cars

One of the most interesting jobs I ever had was driving the police car. There were two black drivers at that time in Cedar Rapids, and in the summer when they were on vacation, I'd get to take over.

Chief of police Benesh liked me and treated me like a grownup. He'd come in first thing in the morning and say, "Cecil, let's go out and dig up some shrubbery." I soon learned that what we were really going to do was dig up the alcohol that bootleggers had buried the night before in different places on the outskirts of town. I don't know how he knew where to look, but we always found something. He must have had some really good inside information.

The very first call I had as a driver was on a bank robbery. We jumped into the big bullet-proof car called a Terra Plane, which was made by the Essex Company. The detectives were all loading their guns as we took off. They told me, "Cecil, when we get to the bank, don't stop. Just slow down and let us jump. Then wait about a block away." I said, "Don't worry about me stopping. You guys just get off as fast as you can." Well, we got there, and I moved through so fast I hardly saw anything. I waited *several* blocks away. It turned out to be a false alarm, but that didn't keep my heart from pounding for an hour later.

I also used to hose down all the cells in the jail and feed the prisoners. There was one prisoner in particular who always used to menace me as I performed these tasks. I had to take him from the courtroom back to his cell and lock him up. He'd bragged that he would someday make a break and that I wouldn't be able to stop him. Finally, I told one of the black policemen who was a former fighter. He was a big husky man who roomed at our house. The next day he took off his badge and gun and went into the cell. He said, "Why don't you break out now?" He gave the bully a lesson in fighting.

Snake Hips

But the best moneymaker was show business. My sister and brother and I had an act called the Three Gold Flashes that got to be popular in the area. We all danced and played instruments, but each of us had a specialty. Edie played the piano and sang. Her act was unusual because she'd sing some in Czech, German, or Spanish, depending on the audience.

I used to do a Frankenstein imitation and a toy soldier routine, plus a "snake hips" dance in a shiny sequinned costume with a gold belt. Wally made that costume and most of the others. He also had the fastest dancing feet I've ever seen. He was the business head in the act, deciding when, where, and for how much we'd work.

Our steadiest gig was for Dempsey Jones's Hillbilly Band. Jones was a white man from South Carolina who had a group with his three sons. He played the guitar, one son played a bass viol, another a getune, and the third played a very odd instrument. It was an empty tub turned upside down with a broomstick resting on top of it. The broomstick had a long heavy piece of rubber innertube attached to it. This contraption sounded like a bass.

We constantly changed things in our routine so that it seemed to get better all the time. We sure put in long hours though, going to school in the daytime, doing chores, and shining shoes. We'd drive up to a hundred miles for an evening performance, then start back home about midnight. There weren't any driver's tests

We called our dance act the Three Gold Flashes because in our finale, we appeared under flashing lights in gold costumes which my brother Wally had made. I'm on the right in this picture with sister Edie in the middle and Wally on the left.

in those days, and a license was only fifty cents. I was just a kid, but I drove in all kinds of stormy weather. If we hadn't been young and loved what we were doing, we'd never have made it.

We adapted our act to the audience. When we danced for whites in some towns, Edie dressed sort of like Aunt Jemima and Wally and I as cooks or waiters. But when we appeared in black

Edie and I always opened our act for white audiences in these costumes. Dressing like servants seemed to open the door for us; then we could go on to flashier clothes and stunts. I used to tap dance holding Edie over my head.

theaters or big cities, we wore extra-flashy costumes, and I'd jump from the balcony onto the stage and land in a split!

As the three of us got older and our lives changed, the act changed again and again. Wally moved to California. Edie and I danced together for a time until she got married. I danced alone until a guy named Jack Brinkley from St. Louis became my part-

When I got a little older and Edie and Wally were involved in other activities, I partnered with Jack Brinkley, a fantastic dancer and nice guy. We did a lot of precision dancing and used to "challenge" each other, taking turns trying to outdo the other.

ner for a while. He had a tremendous personality and a beautiful big grin. What a tap dancer he was. He could dance as well sitting down as most could standing.

We worked in many small towns, mainly for the American Legion, the Elks Club, and the unions. We'd perform at their dinners and dances. The women would fix these big dinners, then we'd sing and dance for about an hour before they'd have their dance. They'd pay us $10 to $20 apiece plus mileage—a lot of money to us in those days. I got a kick out of the way Jack talked sometimes. He loved fried chicken. When they'd ask him what kind of meat he wanted, he'd say, "Give me some of them bresses," meaning chicken breasts.

Shiny Shoes

Although I'd shined shoes here and there earlier, when I was in high school I started working for Mr. Overall making some real money at it. He had the shoeshine concession at the Roosevelt Hotel in Cedar Rapids. The Rock Island Railroad ran football and basketball specials. People who wanted to attend the University of Iowa games in Iowa City would charter an entire train for the weekend. Because Iowa City had so few hotels, most people would stay in Cedar Rapids. So I worked with three other guys in the Roosevelt's twelve-chair shoeshine stand. My older brother Jim and I and the Gibson brothers, Powell and Olin, would shine shoes for Mr. Overall on Friday evening, all-day Saturday, and Sunday morning and make about $16 each. Powell and I were especially close, and his untimely death a few years later hurt me a lot. But the four of us working together as a team made shoe shining a profitable and enjoyable experience.

People would just pile in there. We'd shine shoes so long we could hardly straighten our backs up. At the time, we thought it was awfully tough, but it made us strong. We were probably stronger than the guys on the school's football team. It really strengthened our arms and upper body.

It seems to me that blacks have always added a little something to their work. I don't know whether it was because you had to be a little unusual to get opportunities or whether we just like to have things fancier. Similar to the black construction workers I mentioned earlier, we developed little flourishes in the way we'd shine shoes that were unique and entertaining. Of course we'd get bigger tips, but I think it also made the work more satisfying. It might be, too, that it was a way of being in control of your life. You might have to do what you were told, but no one could fault you for doing it with style and much better than most. Being unique made you more acceptable; being better than most at what you did put you ahead of the curve.

So we learned a lot from shining shoes. Mr. Overall would talk to us from time to time about how to dress and behave to get the biggest tips. Then, too, we overheard news about business and learned how college alumni talk about business and investments. In general, we got a picture of how the buttermilk looks from the inside.

Good Sports

Most of my friends and I were too busy to be involved in sports at school. We'd fight for money, though, when boxing matches were held in town. They had what were called "battle royals" in which five guys would fight in one ring and the last one still standing got the most money, sometimes as much as $100.

The only other time we could play sports was on Sunday afternoon—and that was just for fun. We'd play baseball and horseshoes at Riverside Park by the starch factory and in Sinclair Park by the packinghouse. Some whites would join us, particularly our Czech neighbors.

Our fancy plays would attract quite a crowd to these games, blacks and whites alike. Some of the guys were so good at hitting and stealing bases that they were a show themselves. George Clark hit a home run every time he came to bat and then ran like the wind. People were amazed at his speed as well as his ability to hit. Other players would pretend they weren't watching when a man was at bat. They'd be looking around, talking to someone in the crowd. Then when the batter hit the ball near them, they'd reach out at the last minute and catch the ball without even looking at it.

We got these ideas from the Kansas City Monarchs, the Texas Black Spiders, and other black teams. There was even a mixed team called the House of David. Even though they were exceptional players, black ballplayers were never allowed to play in the white minor or major leagues. Once blacks were admitted, a few of the old-time players made it into the major leagues. For instance, Satchel Paige played until he was past fifty. He had amazing stamina. He could pitch doubleheaders that went into extra innings. I don't think any but his closest Kansas City friends knew his age.

White Beauty Work

As I moved into my later teens, I continued washing windows, cutting grass, and changing storm windows and screens for people, but I got involved in regular jobs that taught me new skills. I worked for a white woman named Helen Dennie who had a business called the Barber and Beauty Shop, a beauty parlor for white people. I started out cleaning the shop for her but was soon making the hairset and shampoo solutions and being the general fix-it man. When she expanded to three other locations, I installed the plumbing, mirrors, lights, etc.

I also taught Helen's daughter, Jackie, to tap dance. She was starstruck and wanted to add tap dancing to her list of talents. But she never became a performer. She must have had her mother's business mind because she ended up managing a large theater in New York and later in Chicago. As I look back now, I wonder why it was never a problem for a young black man to be teaching dance to a young white woman. Dancing involves close touching, but it seemed real natural at the time. I think the people at the shop regarded me as a friend, not just a shoe shiner and porter. I believe they thought of me as someone similar to Bill "Bojangles" Robinson in the Shirley Temple movies that were so popular in those days.

Helen never minded asking the most from you. She didn't want the hot-water heater running all night, so she told me to go in each morning at four to turn the hot-water tank on to insure the water would be warm by eight. My days were long enough as it was, so I invented an automatic timer. I soldered a spoon to an alarm clock. As the clock unwound, the spoon would push the hot-water "on" switch at 4 A.M. while I was fast asleep at home. I never told her about my invention and took it with me when I left there.

Helen paid me $5 per week to clean the beauty shop which

was half a block long, and then I'd make some extra money shining shoes. When she opened a new shop in other towns, she'd give me $15 or $20 for each depending upon how many chairs and mirrors I had to install. She always had everything ready to go when we got there. She'd drive me to the shop, and we'd eat lunch in a nearby restaurant. There was never any problem with that—either because the local people knew her or because she was obviously much older than I.

It seemed odd to me in those days, and it still does, that white people spend so much time, effort, and money trying to get their hair as curly as blacks while blacks had beauty shops that took the curl *out* of your hair. This process was called conking and was sort of a permanent wave in reverse. The chemicals used for this process were terribly harsh, and if you weren't careful they'd eat up your hair and scalp.

Helen's shop was all-white, and there weren't any official black beauty shops in the area. In fact, there were no licensing requirements in those days. So you took your chances. There were always black women who got to be known for being good at "doing hair," so most black women would go to them. But men got their hair conked, too. One of my friends was having his hair conked by a barber who made his own solutions. The barber put too much strong soap in it and left it on too long before using a vinegar rinse to neutralize it. When he took the little skull cap off that held the chemicals into the hair, all of my friend's hair came off with it—sort of like one big scab. It took six months for his hair to grow back.

Harm's Way Lessons

I think one reason I was able to stay out of harm's way during this vulnerable time in my life was my busy schedule. I was always busy, always productive. Grown-ups were impressed by my hard work, so they encouraged and helped me. I found that white people would put their prejudice aside if you did the job. I used to pretend these businesses were mine, and I think that helped me do a better job. It also made boring or rough work more enjoyable. In addition, I learned how important window dressing is.

Dressing very, very sharp makes you stand out and welcome in any company. And the good feeling you get when you know people like the way you look gives you self-confidence. One seems to support the other. I think this is why it's so important for youngsters to have nice clothes, to take an interest in them.

Being in harm's way taught me to feel my way through each situation, to be on the alert, to measure people and their attitudes by their responses to you. I'd watch people's reactions when the Klan was mentioned or racial jokes told. This sensitivity to what was going on with other people's emotions helped me monitor my own actions and reactions. And I learned patience, that it might take a little longer to get what you wanted, but you *could* eventually get it. This is difficult for teenagers to practice, and I guess that's why I think it was so important to learn at that time of my life.

By the time I was twenty, I knew how to maneuver my way through the buttermilk. Truthfully though, I can never completely get over the fear of being in harm's way. Blacks know this feeling of constantly being on the alert. One reason I don't drink or use other drugs is that they cloud your mind. You might miss seeing the signal go from green to yellow to red! But if you learn the signals and refine the God-given sensitivity we all have, harm's way can be a time and place for preparing yourself for the next important phase in your life. That's what it did for me.

5 Show Business at Home and on Stage

Even though blacks in small midwestern towns were few in number and miles away from big-city black neighborhoods, we saw our share of entertainers. During the twenties and thirties black musicians and entertainers were in constant demand in white hotels, nightclubs, and theaters. Like boxing, it was a reliable way to make big money. Notice I didn't say easy because these black entertainers constantly faced danger and discomfort as they traveled from city to city and from town to town. They were not allowed to stay in the hotels where they entertained; they were not allowed to eat in most restaurants. So enterprising black families in rural areas would rent rooms to these traveling entertainers and serve them meals. And long after the fancy hotels and restaurants opened up to them, such greats as Louis Armstrong continued to stay with black families. Many blacks in remote areas maintained extra-large homes just for this purpose. It was a way of making money and keeping up with the times. You could learn so much by hosting these sophisticated, talented, traveled people. Besides, it was exciting and fun. The room-and-board arrangements for black entertainers were made by each theater manager who kept lists of good homes. They had a whole network of people to call on when shows were coming to town.

A constant stream of entertainers came to the Cedar Rapids area. For such a little town as it was then, we got more than our share of shows. Maybe it was because we had lots of different kinds of places for entertainment. The Majestic Theater was an opera house that brought in the minstrel shows. The Iowa and Paramount theaters attracted vaudeville acts and big bands. And the Shrine Temple housed Broadway shows. There were even a couple of dance halls that black groups like the Kappa and Alpha fraternity and sorority could rent occasionally for big band dances of our own.

Star Boarders

Keeping these show business greats was a tradition with the Reed family that my folks started when I was a kid and that my wife and I continued when we had our own home. Mom always kept the extra rooms clean and ready for guests, so she'd just have to buy the food for the big hearty meals she served. The Reed hospitality got to be well known by such showpeople as Louis Armstrong, Duke Ellington, Blanche and Cab Calloway, and Sonny Price. They counted on "Julia Reed's pies" when they were in Cedar Rapids. When the great saxophonist and bandleader Coleman Hawkins would arrive in town, one of the first things he did was to call our house and tell Mom which of his favorite dishes he wanted her to make. Usually it was neckbones and beans or ham and greens with corn bread.

We were on a first-name basis with Count Basie, Jimmy Lunceford, Noble Sissle, the Four Cleffs, the Step Brothers, the Nicholas Brothers, the King Cole Trio, and Louie Jordan and his Timpany Five. One of my favorite groups was the Nicholas Brothers. I always felt excited when I saw them. They were so energetic, they'd dance right up the wall. They used their hands in the act in a graceful way that really made them unique. Another unusual guy was Peg Leg Bates, a fine tap dancer with one wooden leg. One of the best "sand man" dancers, Eddie Rector, was a regular at our house, too.

Other lesser-known but equally talented black artists stayed with us: Dog Woods, Speck Red, Eli Rice, the Sweethearts of Rhythm (the first all-female band I ever saw), and James Weldon Johnson, the poet, songwriter, and diplomat who wrote "O Black and Unknown Bards." Johnson was the first black admitted to the Florida bar and was one of the founders and a secretary of the National Association for the Advancement of Colored People.

A white couple, Don and Mazie Dixon, were also regulars. They'd heard about how nice and clean my mother kept the house and how good her cooking was. So they called and came out and said they wanted to board with us when their stock company was in town. We were surprised that white people wanted to stay in a black home, but it proved to be a wonderful friendship. They almost became like family to us. When they'd be off in some other section of the country for a while, they'd always stay in contact by phone and letters.

Don was the funniest comedian I've ever seen. He played the lovable fool, and Mazie was the beautiful rich lady or the innocent young thing. He wrote all their material. Their stock company traveled all over and regularly came to Iowa. They did plays kind of like the sitcoms of today. They worked with us on improving our act and taught us about the business side of show business. Wally was their favorite, and they taught him a lot about booking shows, negotiating money, developing contacts, and keeping records.

Sometimes you met show people only a time or two, but you'd hear their names later and know they were still in the business. There was one bass player named John Levy who just seemed to disappear. He was a tall, good-looking black man who was a fine dresser. I've often wondered if he is the same John Levy who became George Shearing's manager.

Minstrel Shows

I got my first taste of show business on the *Morning Star* show-boat back when we lived in Davenport. What a thrill at five or six in the evening to see the side of the riverboat let down and become a stage with bright lights and colorful settings. Blacks in brilliantly colored costumes would come out to sing and dance. Minstrel shows on Broadway and other large cities were whites in blackface, but the *Morning Star* had only black performers. When I became old enough to think about it, I realized how strange the history of these shows is. Historians theorize that the cakewalk originated when plantation servants imitated whites doing the minuet. Then a few generations later, through minstrel shows, the cakewalk became the "in" dance in high society.

The American version of the minstrel show had its roots in the juba, a plantation dance in slavery times which was held on New Year's Day. Slaves exchanged homemade gifts, feasted, and danced to the accompaniment of handclapping, rattling bones, and often a banjo or a violin. The minstrel players took the juba dance off the plantation, smoothed it up, and introduced it all over America and Europe where it was at its zenith in popularity by the 1840s. Even though most minstrel shows featured all-white casts in blackface cork, the best-known minstrel player was William Henry Lane, a freeborn black from Providence, Rhode Island. He had a reputation as a jig dancer, so when big-time minstrel shows took on mixed casts, he worked with the best and soon had top billing as "Mr. Juba."

Besides discovering an appreciation for drama and glamour from watching these shows, seeing blacks perform so well was particularly meaningful to me. When growing up in an area where most of your role models were white, it helped to know that there were many talented, successful blacks who were famous worldwide. One of the most inspiring performers I've ever seen was Marian Anderson. She was so admired that when she came to Cedar Rapids before the civil rights laws were passed, she was allowed to stay at the Roosevelt Hotel. But the catch was that she had to ride the freight elevator up to her room because the hotel was afraid her presence would hurt their business. This kind of discrimination was so common it was accepted without protest. Just her getting to stay at the hotel was a victory.

There are many other ironies regarding blacks and entertainment. Whites chose to believe slaves sang out of simpleminded happiness. In fact, slave songs had two levels, one musical and one communication. Whites thought that the house blacks and field people did not get along. In fact, they used slave songs to send each other messages. By singing "far, far away" the house blacks might be telling the field blacks "the master's gone, so you can worship." On the other hand, the field blacks might sing "I'm coming, I'm coming" when they saw the master approaching the plantation, thus allowing the house blacks to finish any banned activities.

Lessons from Show Business

I learned some pretty important ideas and skills from my early experiences with show business. Listening to these people talk kind of filled in the details about things we'd read about in black newspapers. They told us the stories behind the stories. They also told us where to eat and stay and what to see when we went to the cities. These entertainers helped prepare us for the sight of big, thriving communities filled with black businesses and accommodations. It excited our young minds to know there were places where blacks were in the majority. Black entertainers whetted our appetites to visit there and showed us how to act when we got there.

We learned a lot about interpersonal relations from them, too. They set a model for being polite and sophisticated: stepping aside for the ladies to enter the door, how to answer impolite people when they said or did something insulting, and how to make your point without getting angry and angering others. Just the fact that these internationally known stars would take the time to watch us do our acts made us feel good. Then, too, they'd add little touches to our singing, dancing, and playing that made all the difference in the world. What's more, they inspired and encouraged us to stay with it.

I think that having some entertainment skills is good for anyone providing you don't have to be "on" all the time. It gives you confidence to be able to sing a song, do an imitation, play the piano, or tell a story in a dramatic way. People are glad to have you around when you can do something that makes them laugh or entertains them. We were lucky in our family to have advice from some of the world's greatest performers. But I'm most grateful for how they helped me develop my skills as a speaker. Because of them I learned how to relate to an audience so that I could speak from my heart to many people about the ideas and feelings most important to me.

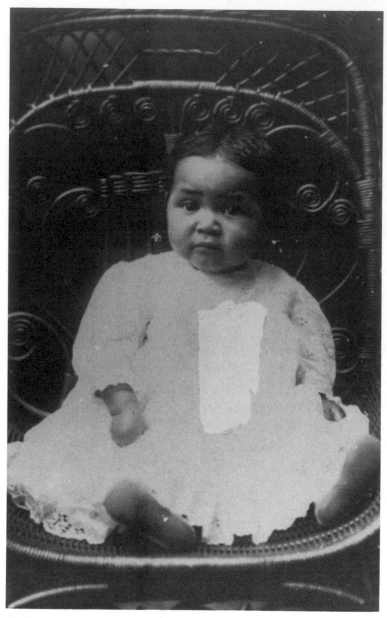

Evelyn, my wife, when she was a baby. She was born in Minneapolis, Minnesota, in 1912.

6   Honing Life Skills

In 1933 when I was not quite twenty, I met Evelyn Collins, the daughter of an African Methodist Episcopal (AME) minister in Cedar Rapids who had recently come from Minnesota. It was a big happening in the black community to have a new minister move in.

The adults wondered what kind of preacher he'd be; the young people wondered if there'd be new social activities and what the Collins's four children (Evelyn, Charlotte, John Wesley, and

Jimmy) would be like. And I was just one of the black guys who was surveying those two beautiful young ladies who'd entered our social circle.

As I think back to those busy days, I wonder how I had time to fall in love. But then I remember how strong and full of energy I was *and* how I felt the first time I saw Evelyn. The second Sunday after the Collins family came to Cedar Rapids, I met Evelyn at church. I felt she was the woman for me from the very start and set out to make it possible to marry her someday. I began to walk her home from church and other functions, then escorted her to parties and dances.

When Evelyn and I were young dating was quite different than it is today. We walked almost everywhere. Most of our activities were nearby, and everyone walked. But when functions were held in other towns, we'd find a way to attend. Sometimes we'd double-date or triple up with friends who owned cars or borrowed them from their folks. Other times I'd drive Dad's car, an old Buick. Neither he nor Mom knew how to drive, but Dad bought a license each year. I did the family driving for as long as I can remember, but I never owned a car of my own until I was married.

We'd hire a white man named Frank to drive us for those special occasions when we'd all buy corsages for our dates and really dress up. Frank had a Kissell car he used as a taxi. He'd charge $1.25 to drive you downtown. If you double-dated, you could split that in half. When there was an important event coming up, Frank made a schedule ahead of time so that all of us had a chance to go by taxi. But most of the time we walked everywhere. We talked and had such a good time, we'd be there before we knew it. That's the way it is when you're in love.

I knew that in the African Methodist Episcopal church the ministers are transferred to other towns about every three or four years. So it was always a concern in the back of my mind that she might move away before I was in a position to ask her to marry me. She was very pretty, and there was enough competition at home without having to contend with a long-distance romance. One day my fears were realized when her dad announced he had been transferred to the AME church in Davenport, Iowa. For about a year, I took the train every weekend to Davenport to see her. It was time-consuming, and I had to worry about all the competition in Davenport. So I asked her parents if we could get married. I jokingly told them that commuting was getting expensive and that it would be cheaper to take her home with me. They consented, and so did she. We were married in her home by her father.

My folks were happy about our marriage. Ev and I had been courting almost three years, and they liked her and her parents. Since her father had been our minister for a while, they knew the entire family pretty well. In fact, we lived with my parents at 711 Tenth Street for the first six months we were married. We took over the house payments and eventually paid it off. When Evelyn became pregnant with our first child, Carol, she was ill all the time. She wanted to be with her mother, so we moved to Davenport and lived with her parents.

I got a job in Davenport at the YMCA health club. I learned to do massage and monitor the steam cabinets and electric baths. I was also the lifeguard during swimming lessons. I put in a shoeshine stand to make a little extra money on the side. Although I'd always worked hard at several jobs at a time, I was really motivated now that there was a baby on the way.

Integrating the Maternity Ward

When Ev's labor started and I took her to the hospital, we noticed there was a white woman in labor, too. In those days, black and white patients were separated, so they were in different rooms connected by a nurses' station. This woman's husband was nowhere to be seen, so I kept running back and forth between the two rooms trying to cheer and help them both. The white woman couldn't believe that black husbands were so attentive to births. She said, "He's actually looked out for both of us." She had her family send Evelyn a big bouquet of flowers. The doctor was so impressed, he started coming to the health club at the YMCA where I worked.

While shining shoes in Cedar Rapids, I'd met a man named Jim Yuhl who was in the real-estate business. When he learned we wanted to buy a small house in Cedar Rapids, he told me he

Evelyn and I met when her father became the minister of the Cedar Rapids African Methodist Episcopal Church in 1933. He married us a few years later. She studied child psychology at Coe College, Cedar Rapids, and bore our four children, Carol, Dick, Mike, and David. She did the bookwork and money management for our various businesses in the Cedar Rapids area and was active in many church and civic groups.

had one on the south side of Mt. Zion Baptist Church (black) for $1,500. He carried the contract on it and asked for a $125 down payment. I thought this was rather high at the time. But I had some savings from making pretty good money at the Elks and from the extra cleaning and entertaining I'd done. So, soon after the birth, we went back to Cedar Rapids and settled into our own two-bedroom house at 826 Eighth Street. The Elks gave us all kinds of beautiful baby furniture for Carol's room. They painted the room and hung pink wallpaper with cute little animals all over it. They even provided diapers!

The kitchen was very small and was equipped with apartment-sized appliances, so I painted it pure white. The house had a front porch with a swing and a tiny backyard. Grass wouldn't grow back there because it was heavily shaded, so I converted it to a Chinese tea garden. The furniture store gave me the big cane poles that come in carpet rolls, and I used them to make a cane fence and furniture. I put pea gravel on the ground and planted some oriental-looking flowers and shrubs, then added Chinese lanterns. Some people used to come just to sit back there and think because it was so beautiful and peaceful. So at twenty-three, Ev and I were parents, living in our own house and beginning our own family.

Block Boy

Shortly after I returned to work for Helen Dennie, a white man named Bill Merritt asked me to be the night dishwasher at his restaurant, which was located next to the State Theater. This was a chance for extra money, so I accepted. A little later, he asked me if I could cook. I said, "Sure." Even though I'd never cooked in a restaurant, I'd done plenty of it at home.

Anyway, I became a "block boy"—which is like a short-order cook. Only in this restaurant you really had to be quick—or short with the orders. Because the restaurant was located at a bus stop, most of the customers were in a big hurry. We had two menus and two ways of preparing the food. For the rush orders, there was a special stove that the block boy cooked on. It was an electric stove that was right behind the counter. It had heat from below and above. You'd put on ham, chops, or steaks and then pull the top down close for super-fast cooking.

After I'd been a block boy for a while, the chef left, and Mr. Merritt asked me if I could be a chef. Again, I said "sure" and *then* learned to be a chef. Sometimes I was all three—dishwasher, block boy, and chef. The other block boys were white and were involved in school athletics. When they took off to practice or play, I'd sometimes work night and day to make extra money. Besides, I liked the feeling of being able to handle anything that came my way.

Busy Evelyn

Evelyn was pretty busy herself. During that time, she worked at the Three Sisters dress shop in downtown Cedar Rapids as a window decorator and "bushellman," a term that was used for someone who alters clothing. It was the second level before you could be a journeyman tailor. Ev's sister took care of Carol while Ev worked. Evelyn enjoyed the work and was very good at it, but her hours were long and inconvenient.

More Jobs

I moved over to Old Hickory, a nightclub and bar on the highway between Cedar Rapids and Marion. On Monday I'd make barbecue for the week and put it in a big walk-in icebox. The rest of the week I was the cook. Sometimes I'd be a waiter during dinner, then late in the evening I'd put on a costume and perform in a tap dance act with Edie and Wally.

I always liked to keep the kitchen clean, so I even cleaned the smokestack over the barbecue. One day I was stretching up to clean the inside way up high and lost my footing. I fell on one of the iron rods of the barbecue and impaled my rib cage on it. There was no one around to help me, and I hung there for some time until I finally made one gigantic effort to lift myself off. I just wrapped a towel and the apron around the wound and kept on working. When Mr. Harger, the owner of the club, noticed it later in the day, he really gave me the dickens for not telling anyone and then sent me to the hospital.

At the same time, Edie, Wally, and I were entertaining at the Elks Club. Edie had started as a hatcheck girl and soon got us all working there at different tasks. Eventually we ended up being a crew that would not only serve food, tend bar, and entertain, but we cleaned up afterward. Sometimes the members would have us cater parties in their homes, and I got floor maintenance jobs from them, too.

Wally was very creative and articulate. He sounded like a Harvard graduate and looked like a million dollars. He'd buy an expensive suit at the secondhand store no matter what size it was and cut it down to fit him. He knew how to make the food look attractive with open-faced sandwiches, elegant hors d'oeuvres, and fancy trays. Because of these experiences, I was eventually asked to work at the Elks Club. Basically, I did everything: I was the bartender, waiter, and maintenance man. I also did all kinds of cleaning and even refinished the hardwood floors. I made a lot of money—but they got a bargain.

Sometimes I'd make some extra money with sort of a "hustle" my boss set up. He would hint around that he knew someone who could carry the club's great big upright piano down the stairs alone. The Elks were betting people, and soon someone would challenge him to put his money where his mouth was. I'd walk up, take the wheels off, brace myself up against the handrail, then slide the piano down the steps. I'd get half the money he collected from the bets. Four maintenance men would take the piano back up the steps on Monday.

The Foxhead Tavern

One member of the Elks, Rod Kenyon, asked me to run his bar. It was the Foxhead Tavern, the longest bar in the state of Iowa. We could only serve beer there, but the bar really prospered. Even though it was not the thing to do in Iowa, Rod allowed blacks to be bar patrons. They had to sit in a special section, but still, it was a step forward. Rod paid me well and hired Ev to come and clean the glasses. This helped a lot, because the

Here's how Nat King Cole looked when he appeared at the Foxhead Tavern in Cedar Rapids, the longest bar in Iowa, where I served as talent scout, electrician, bartender, maintenance man, and substitute manager when the owner went into the navy in World War II. I spotted Nat performing in a showbar across from the Chicago Theater and booked him for the Foxhead.

work she'd been doing at the Three Sisters involved long hours. At the Foxhead, she worked less but was paid more. It was good for me, too, because I learned about the money management side of business and how show business operates behind the scenes.

I cleaned, ordered, and went to Chicago to contact entertainers. The tavern was kind of a showbar with bands. Rod let me hire all of his bands from a guy named Beryl Adams, who later became a big-time agent. Several times I put Beryl on to talent. For instance, I saw a new trio working in a little showbar in Chicago . . . the King Cole Trio. I told Beryl how good they were and that he ought to take them on. Well, Beryl did, and he became Nat's agent, an arrangement that lasted until Nat died. Beryl's company was called Mutual Casting Agency (MCA). I wonder if it became MCA, today's giant music management company. It makes me smile to think that we hired Nat King Cole at the Foxhead at a time when we had to pay much more for Coleman Hawkins, who was already popular when Beryl was handling him.

King's Conk

Nat was businesslike and serious about his work. He smiled a lot but wasn't a big laugher. However, he still had a good sense of humor about himself as this story will attest. The solution Nat used for conk jobs made his scalp itch when he perspired. So when he'd be performing under those hot lights, he'd scratch his head quite a bit. I could do a good King Cole voice, so I'd imitate him backstage, alternating song phrases with head scratches: "I realize now (scratch, scratch) . . . how my eyes could have been so blind (scratch, scratch) . . . I can't help loving you (scratch, scratch) . . ." One night, several of his musicians caught me and insisted I repeat it to Nat. Luckily, he was pretty amused.

I also made boarding arrangements for the musicians and helped get tavern commercials made for radio. The radio station where we advertised would record one full song by each talent appearing at the tavern. We'd keep these recordings for Beryl to hear so he could see whom he wanted to represent as an agent.

I wired the tavern, upstairs and down, with a sound system which I built with some plywood and a couple of old jukeboxes. I arranged it so that from his office in the basement, Ron could both control and monitor what was being played. We played records during the group's intermissions.

Cecil's Band

About that time I put together a small band and a troupe of dancers. So I was playing bass in my own band and running the tavern. Sometimes my group would get gigs at other places, usually after-hours black clubs. I'd work late afternoons and the evenings at the tavern, then take my band to perform at the American Legion or the Hi Ho Tavern up the street. We had a banner that was a takeoff on the song that went, "Rings on her fingers, bells on her toes, for she shall have music wherever she goes." My version said, "Cece shall have music wherever he goes."

Rod was an abrasive character, but he'd let you have full rein. You could have a lot of responsibility, learn a lot from it, and be well paid. He expected a lot out of you, and he got it from me. So it was a rewarding experience for both of us. It was during this period that I learned how to organize my work, myself, and my time, so that later on I would be able to train and manage others in my own business. I was honing the skills I already had so that I could be a successful entrepreneur.

During this same period, I began servicing jukeboxes. I had a regular route and would get a percentage on the records I put in. I also sold the used records. The jukebox business inspired me to think of "Cecil's Make Believe Band," a business that got the whole family involved. I knew there were many groups that couldn't afford to hire a band for their parties, so I'd rent a dance hall, play records, and do a little talking—disco style. Years later a guy came along and did the same thing and made a fortune on it—Dick Clark and his American Bandstand. But he didn't have Ev to serve barbecue. We had our own PA system and a whole range of entertainment services we could offer. We'd make it a real occasion for our clients, so we were scheduled for almost every holiday and weekend.

All the Reed siblings were developing business skills during that period. Wally and Lulu were catering, and Ev and I would help out when we weren't too busy. We all worked hard, but it hardly seemed like work. It was so exciting and challenging to be learning new things, developing better ways of doing what we already knew how to do, that I think we all had a great sense of hope and eagerness for the future.

Ev and I would soon have another child, Richard. We were young and energetic and beginning to become valued members of the community. We were highly visible flies in the buttermilk— and welcome company in most places.

7 Bracing the System

During the war years, Ev and I were busy with our growing young family, an active social life, and many business projects. After Dick was born on September 18, 1943, we began thinking about buying a larger home. We had some money put aside thanks to Evelyn. She was very good at handling finances; she made sure the bills were paid on time, which established good credit. She saw to it that we saved some money as we went along, too. Our grocer, Alex Homsey, a Lebanese man who lived on the other side of the church, sold us his house for $3,800. We put $1,500 down, and the Bohemian Savings and Loan carried the rest. Located at 814 Eighth Street, this was a large two-story house with a full basement, a beautiful grape arbor, and a three-car garage. After we moved to the larger house, Ev and I would have a big party once a year. We'd hire Wally, my brother, to prepare the food because he made delicious, elaborate foods such as chicken tetrazzini, and he set a beautiful table. Because this and our later houses were all roomy, I'd fix the basements up with a jukebox, a place to dance, and game machines. Black friends from all parts of the state would drive down for the party, and many would spend the night. Once a year in the summertime, we'd have a picnic for blacks *and* whites. It changed over the years, but in the beginning, whites would not have been comfortable coming to a party inside a black's house.

Since both Ev and I came from religious families, our social life was within the church and our families. Mother was very active in fund-raisers, and Dad attended church twice every Sunday. Ev and I were always busy with church activities, and we kept our children involved in the church from the time they were little.

Evelyn took good care of the house and children. She liked to dress the kids in the finest-looking fashions that young people were wearing so they'd never feel different. She felt that being black was already a visible strike against them, so why not make it as easy as possible by always being clean, neat, and in fashion. I guess, too, it's natural to want your kids to have more than you had when you were growing up.

I took the family swimming and boating quite often since I loved the water and fancied myself to be a good swimmer. We'd picnic by ourselves and with other families, mostly from the church.

Busy Work

We were equally involved in earning a living. In addition to working for other people, I'd started a floor maintenance business that we operated out of the three-car garage. Eventually it became

We ran this ad to announce the opening of the Floor Care Store.

our main livelihood. I'd gotten started in floor maintenance through the skills I gained and the people I met at the Elks Club. I learned the basics and got my original customers there. It began small with just scrubbing and waxing floors and gradually grew into a sizable operation. Soon, I had both the hospitals in town,

When we opened Reed's Floor Care Store, we had everything spic-and-span.

St. Luke's and Mercy, three or four hotels, and many homes for accounts.

At times, Jeannie Walker Mitchell, my niece, was the secretary. At first, my son, Dick, and I did most of the work but as business grew we'd hire young people to help us. Years later, when it became a full-time operation, we had three full-time lead workers: Dick; my son-in-law, Ted Hughes; and Noble Woods, a friend. They'd train, supervise, and work right along with the crews. Initially, we hired a professional bookkeeping service to set up the books, and then Ev ran it. We'd have ten to fifteen workers, off and on, many of them from the families of our Czechoslovakian friends.

I had a special crew that removed old floor coverings and refinished floors. That was probably the most lucrative part of my business. Removing the old tile and linoleum was hard, dirty work that nobody wanted to do. But we accidentally found an easy, fast way of doing it. One crew had a string of jobs in buildings that weren't heated in the winter. They noticed how easy it was to get the tile up in these frigid places. So when we had a tile removal project we'd get big boxes of dry ice, cover the floor, and the tile would just jump off the floor.

With a lot of hard work and a little advertising, the business thrived. One of our ads said, "Save overhead underfoot; if you keep the floor clean, it cuts down on cleaning the rest of the home or office." Ultimately, we had three floor operations: Reed's Floor Store in Cedar Rapids where we sold supplies, Reed's Floor Maintenance for cleaning and repair, and Reed's Floor Sanding and Finishing business.

Ev and I learned a lot about real estate from buying our own homes. Eventually, that led us into another enterprise: buying properties, fixing them up, and then renting or selling them. I'd finish the basements in these houses and put in a recreation room complete with music speakers. We called them whoopy basements in those days. Now you'd call them family rooms. Those houses would sell in a hurry because people loved the basements.

Moving On

When Evelyn became pregnant with Michael (born September 10, 1948), we decided to move to the country. We wanted room for the kids to roam and a quiet place for my parents to live. This sounds like a major move, but actually we were looking for something just a few miles out of Cedar Rapids and eventually found it.

Even though we were well established as honest, hardworking businesspeople, no one in the all-white area we liked would sell to us. In fact, I heard that some people even got up a petition to prevent our moving there. I wasn't really offended by this because I understood that the whites felt threatened. They disguised it by claiming they were concerned about their property values. They were kidding themselves. They just weren't ready to live next door to blacks. We were determined to move in anyway, but we decided to do everything possible to help them feel comfortable with us.

Finally, we were able to buy a piece of property from Walt Ellerton, a white fellow I'd known since the days when I shined shoes in the same Cedar Rapids shop where he was a barber. He

When we moved to this home at 1120 Bertram Road on fifteen acres at the edge of Cedar Rapids in 1953, we weren't all that welcome. But when we left there later, the neighbors almost didn't let us go.

later became a realtor. The property was located at the edge of Cedar Rapids and had two houses on it. My parents lived in one, and my family moved into the larger house. Davey was born a few years later (June 3, 1952), and over the next twenty years we added rooms and improvements to both houses, turned two acres into a park, and built a motel with two large buildings and five two-room cabins.

Moving to the country gave us plenty of room to expand our rental properties and reorganize the floor maintenance businesses. We converted the home we'd moved out of into three apartments. A few years later we sold it to the Mt. Zion Baptist Church when it expanded. We sold the Tenth Street house that my parents had been living in to a Lebanese man who had his business next door. We continued to rent out our little house on Tenth Street, which we had converted into two small apartments. We bought a building in town that had two storefronts. We rented one to a furnace filter business and used the other for our floor care store. There were two apartments upstairs. The basement was big and held the

Soon after we moved to our place in the country, neighbors helped Dick and me put in a racetrack for quarter midget cars. The cars attracted big crowds, both for the races and for driving safety training. Boys and girls raced and learned mechanical skills. They'd wear white outfits during the races, and some families wore similar clothes to show their pride and support.

equipment we had for the businesses. As bookkeeper, Ev's biggest tasks were payroll and property management. Over the years and at different times, we owned some eighteen houses plus the two business buildings she managed in Cedar Rapids.

Almost every day we improved the country property in some way. We kept everything spotless and neat, and we were careful not to cause a ruckus. I never wanted our kids to bother anyone or feel rejected by whites, so I made our place like an amusement park. We named it Lincoln Park because it was located on the famous old Lincoln Highway. Originally it was a rest stop for Indians and a Cherokee Indian campground. We put in everything a kid would want: slides and swings, a merry-go-round, a trampoline, a tennis court, quarter midget racers, ponies and horses, and a swimming hole at the creek down behind the house.

Some of the fixtures were made from cast-offs. The merry-go-round was an axle off a truck which I stuck in the ground and

Once my family and neighbors had completed the playground, we had a picnic to celebrate. You can see the house and playground in the background. Many people from town joined us.

fastened boards to. Other stuff was given to us, including a trampoline from George Nisson, the founder and president of Nisson Trampoline and a schoolfriend of mine. The Elks Club gave us a Ping-Pong table, a tennis set, tether balls, and a badminton set. We bought old park tables and benches from the city and repaired and painted them.

Then, a funny thing happened. All the white kids began to come over . . . and their parents, too. I guess the neighbors de-

I received this first ever Social Action Award from the Catholic Center Associates for donating land for Lincoln Park and for organizing the project. The award is a ceramic statue of Martín de Porres, a seventeenth-century Afro-Spanish social worker. It was presented by Rev. Edgar Kurt, moderator of the Catholic Center of Cedar Rapids. Cedar Rapids Gazette *photo by Johnny McIvor.*

cided we weren't so bad after all. This was done without harsh words or rancor, without fights and bitterness. I still liked the entertainment business but was too busy to continue with my nightclub performances. Besides, it didn't seem appropriate in the country. So I put together a kids' dance team called "Cecil's Floor Show," using the black children from town. I'd sit in sometimes, playing bass with the band and doing a feature with the dancers.

At the same time we were building our businesses and establishing ourselves as good neighbors, Ev and I were active in community affairs. We'd help out in the community theater, the NAACP annual dinner, and the United Fund. I was the only black businessman in the Chamber of Commerce and eventually became chairman of the chamber. I was the only black on the Cedar Rapids Symphony Board. Later, Ev and I both became

STATE DEPARTMENT CULTURAL EXCHANGE PROGRAM
REPRESENTING SEVEN AFRICAN NATIONS

When the Cedar Rapids Chamber of Commerce worked with the State Department in a cultural exchange program, this group came to our house for a barbecue. We invited the Africans and their interpreters to come back the next day to eat dinner and to play pool. They returned without the interpreters and spoke English. They asked us about how it was to be black in the United States. I explained the difference between small town versus city conditions. They wanted to talk privately with our children; I guess they feared the kids might not feel free to express themselves in front of Ev and me. To this day, I don't know what was said. They talked so long, I finally had to say, "Please let my kids go to bed."

regular speakers at churches and schools on black history and race relations.

I think we also set an example for tolerance that maybe made a difference in some people's attitudes toward minorities. There was a band of gypsies who came to Cedar Rapids every year to fix hydraulic jacks for auto supply stores and garages. They traveled and lived in their own trailers but had a hard time finding a place to park them. I strung up lights on the back of our property and rented them space every year.

They were interesting, enjoyable people. Their trailers were luxurious with deep freezers, rooms that expanded out the sides, and lovely furniture. They were not poor. Nor did they steal as was rumored. They always kept their word with me. They were clean, too. The women used to bathe themselves every day outdoors. They'd hose each other off from head to toe while fully clothed. Very efficient, I thought—they were bathing and doing their laundry at the same time.

In the evenings the gypsies would dance and sing around a campfire. We loved to join them. At first, the neighbors took a dim view of this, but the pretty gypsy women were too much for the local guys to resist. Eventually, there'd be quite a turnout for these evening songfests—and each succeeding year there was less resistance to their camping there.

A Shift in Perspective

As for the Reeds, we became more than welcome in the white community. Sometimes I think they pointed with pride to this successful black family in their midst. And I believe they genuinely liked us. In 1964, Joan Liffring, a reporter and photographer for the *Des Moines Register*, wrote a big article with pictures about our family. Basically, it described the contributions our family had made to the community and the achievements of our children. She and her husband now own Penfield Press in Iowa City, and she is a renowned photographer. The article attracted a great deal of attention and raised our profile in the community. In fact, I believe it was partially responsible for my finally running for office.

Our children were active and accomplished in so many areas that Ev and I couldn't help but be proud of them. Carol was very talented in dancing, singing, and writing and received a lot of attention and awards in those areas. But it seemed to me that she was most excited the time the school newspaper ran a picture of a dress she'd made. The boys were all good athletes and belonged to the Cub Scouts and Boy Scouts, so they were always going to meetings, ball practice, and games. We could never have run all our businesses and kept up with the kids' activities without teamwork. Evelyn took care of such business matters as the phone calls, bookkeeping, income tax, Social Security records, and pay-

This picture of Evelyn and me was part of a large feature article entitled "Small Businessman, Big Citizen," written by Joan Liffring for the Des Moines Sunday Register *in 1964. It described our home, businesses, children, and activities in detail and attracted a lot of attention throughout the state.* Des Moines Register *photo by Joan Liffring.*

roll, while I dealt with the clients, the work projects, and our employees. We shared the cleaning and cooking chores at home. We'd both attend as many of the kids' activities as possible, but lots of times we had to divide those up also.

Gradually, we had become a part of this rural community, partly because the time was right and our neighbors were basi-

The article included this picture of our living room and shows, from left to right, Evelyn on the couch, Mike and Dick standing, Davey working on a puzzle, and me and Carol. Des Moines Register *photo by Joan Liffring.*

cally well-meaning people. But the model we presented as a black family was important, too. When you're a fly in the buttermilk you can be a visible irritant if you aren't careful. We demonstrated that we were honest, hardworking people no different in our hopes than whites. Ev and I didn't spend much time resenting the fact that we all had to go the extra mile to prove ourselves. We were too busy and realistic to waste time and energy on anger and self-pity. You might lose a night's sleep when the kids were affected, but we learned to deal with it and move on. Ultimately, the careful way we'd lived our lives was noticed, and it changed the perspective of the whole community. It wasn't until later that I called it "bracing the system" and started recommending it as a way for the "little person" to make a big difference. I believe that any minority group—whether black, hispanic, gay, or female—must do "bracing" at an individual level if their movement is to progress.

You have to keep a low profile and prove yourself in a hundred different ways. You gain acceptance by being friendly and by

Another picture from the article showed Davey in his fifth-grade classroom at Erskine School. The article described his unhappiness in kindergarten when white children stared at him and said, "You're all black and dirty." Ev and I told him that they had not seen many black people and that they would eventually become his friends. Des Moines Register *photo by Joan Liffring.*

leaving the door open for those who wish to be friendly. You must also be patient and beyond reproach in all your dealings with others. It's like the process of building a house; you install a system of braces that keeps the walls from caving in on you. Little by little, it gets stronger and stronger. Here are some guidelines.

Be honest. We tried to be honest in word and deed. We discussed money in advance so there'd be no misunderstandings. Whenever there was any question, we'd make up the difference financially rather than having someone have any doubts about us. I never said anything I didn't believe to be true.

This picture from the article shows Dick and me working on a floor-sanding project. It mentioned that both of us were members of Carpenter and Joiner's Union, Local 308—the first black members in Cedar Rapids. Des Moines Register *photo by Joan Liffring.*

Dress well, speak well. It is said that most employers decide whether to hire you during the first eight seconds of the job interview. You know that decision is based upon superficial, emotional factors. In any area of social interaction, you are judged in the same quick, emotional way. Add to this the possibility that the other person has a bias against you because of your color, race, nationality, religion, political party, or sexual orientation, and you can see you don't need any external strikes against you. I tell all to save their cool duds and jive talking for Saturday night parties with the brothers and sisters.

Keep a clean, neat home. We were always careful about the appearance of our property because we were aware of the notion among whites that blacks were dirty.

Think of the needs of others. Showing concern and regard for the welfare of all elements of the community makes you feel better about yourself and helps everyone feel like we're all in this together.

Be an interesting, well-informed person. If you are good company, people quickly forget what color you are or other differences between you and them. They become absorbed, instead, with your personality and ideas.

Make your home an inviting place. Lincoln Park attracted first the white children and then adults to our home. Here again, the fun they could have at our home soon obliterated their discomfort about our color.

Take an inch instead of a mile. In 1961, when the civil rights movement was sweeping the country, I wrote a letter to the editor of the *Cedar Rapids Gazette* reassuring residents that blacks moving to Cedar Rapids would maintain a ratio of one black family to a four- or five-block area. The response from whites was relief and gratitude for reasonableness. We could have pushed and demanded, but that would have only made whites fearful and dig in their heels. And it would have undone all the good relations we'd established over years and years.

I know some of these suggestions might sound like "playing the good nigger," but it seems pointless to me to push too far beyond what people are ready to accept. New ideas and ways are never accepted automatically or overnight but are eased into common practice through courageous patience. Also, it takes many different approaches to make broad social changes. The civil rights movement needed dynamic leaders such as the Reverend Martin Luther King, Jr., and Malcolm X; it needed the rebellious Rosa Parks and Black Panthers. But I believe that the progress made by dramatic leaders and incidents always rests upon a foundation of small changes. Our family and thousands of other flies accomplished these essential small changes by the way we lived our daily lives, away from confrontation and headlines.

8   On the Road

Ev and I always traveled as much as circumstances permitted but in different ways at different stages of our lives. We loved our home but always wanted to see other parts of this beautiful country. Before the children came along, we'd visit the big cities to enjoy the excitement of New York's Harlem, Chicago's South Side, Philadelphia's black section, and Los Angeles's Central Avenue. White people told me they were always scared going to these big-city black areas because they'd never seen so many blacks. I felt the same way at first. Remember, I was used to living among whites, so being surrounded by singing, talking, walking, jiving blacks was a little overwhelming. But it didn't take long to get comfortable and feel real good about being part of such a vibrant community full of thriving businesses, all black-owned.

These city blacks were so different; they dressed the same way white showpeople did. The black women were coiffed and fancied up. The men wore Cuban heels and bi-swing-backed suits. Even the little kids had flashy clothes.

Chicago's black section, the South Side, was a splendid city unto itself. It had giant churches and every kind of business imaginable. There were at least twenty black hotels. And New York's was even bigger. The Theresa Hotel was the best in Harlem. Every black star on stage or screen was visible when you walked in there. But we usually stayed at the Cecil Hotel which was frequented mostly by athletes. You'd see the Harlem Globetrotters and the boxers there. And once I saw the Kansas City Monarchs playing a game in slow motion out in front of the hotel. There was no ball, no bat, no umpire, but they made you believe there was a real game going on. Every movement was slow and exaggerated, and they'd make noises to go with it. Maybe it was a way for them to relax before the real thing.

Sugar Ray Makes Way

When we'd go to New York, Ev and I liked to dance at Small's Paradise Club. It was around the corner from the Apollo Theater on Lennox Avenue. If you were good dancers, the crowd would back away, make a big circle around you, and watch you dance. One night when we were there, we ended up in the middle of the floor with only one other couple—Sugar Ray Robinson, the boxer, and his partner. We danced for a while, but then I spun Ev out doing a break and lost my grip on her. She went into the bars in front of the bandstand. She could have ended up in the musicians' laps, but she reached out and I reached out, and we never missed a beat. It just looked like another step. But Sugar Ray knew it wasn't planned. He started laughing and backed off the floor, leaving the spotlight to us.

We liked to go to the famous Apollo Theater where so many black entertainers got started. Next door to the Apollo was a tailor who specialized in rush orders. One day when we were going to a matinee at the Apollo, I ordered two suits, a gray and a white flannel, before we went in. After the show, we had a snack nearby that took just a few minutes. When I went in for the suits, the tailor grumbled at me: "Where have you been? It's been ready for a half hour." I guess we shouldn't have had the snack!

We loved going to the Apollo's amateur shows. The performers all seemed good to me, but the audiences and management were very demanding. They'd pull you off with a sheephook if your act was bad or didn't go over. It was a real risk getting up there. I remember one comedian in particular who had me in stitches but got the hook. He did humor about current events—sort of like Mort Sahl. I guess the audiences at the Apollo weren't yet ready for that kind of material.

The musicians had to be more than just good musicians. They'd embellish their acts with special ways of entering, bowing, and moving their hands. Some would play standing up at the piano or dancing along with the music. And, of course, their costumes were always unique.

Many show business greats such as comedians Nipsey Russell and Redd Foxx got their start through appearances at the Apollo in New York and the Regal in Chicago. And many legendary musicians such as Earl "Fatha" Hines and his band played the Apollo. Billy Eckstine, known for being a great crooner, was a bandleader in those days, playing the valve trombone and singing once in a while. His band spawned the talents of the fine vocalist Sarah Vaughan and sax player Albert Ammonds.

When the acts got big enough, they'd move to the Cotton Club, an elite club for whites. The whites would come to the Apollo, but blacks could not go to the Cotton Club except as entertainers. It was the same way with the Pump Room in Chicago and most other big nightclubs around the country.

Big Cities

We'd visit the big cities one at a time until we got to know them, to know people there. Then we'd take longer trips and make a circuit, dropping off in each place to renew friendships. It was like establishing a route with friendly stops along the way.

You couldn't always find space in black hotels. Besides, they were pretty expensive, so we'd look for "cottages." These were big houses with fourteen and fifteen rooms owned by blacks. Ma Robinson was one well-known owner in Atlantic City. She'd fix great food and serve it family style in a big dining room. It was like a boardinghouse. You'd see the same people over and over again and would go to the clubs and other entertainments with them. It was sort of a "big city" way of doing what the Reeds used to do when they had a boardinghouse for entertainers.

Some of the people in the network we built up while visiting cities were Sugar Ray Robinson, Joe Louis, Sonny Wilson, owner of the Mark Twain Hotel in Detroit, Larry Steele, the nightclub producer for the Paradise Club in Atlantic City, and Joe "Ziggy" Johnson, master of ceremonies at the Rum Boogie Club in Chicago. That's where I heard the best guitar and blues ever from T-Bone Walker. He was also a real showman: the stage would be dark, and a hush would fall over the room as a shaft of light shone on this tall black man dressed in a white tuxedo and playing a white guitar. He'd walk up these white steps, raise his head, and break your heart with "Jelly Roll Blues." He played the electric guitar from his soul and wailed, "Jelly, Jelly, Jelly. Jelly Roll all the time." The whole room reverberated, as the audience beat time on the tables with sticks that management provided. It was quite an experience.

In those days you didn't see beggars on the street or people dealing dope. You felt no fear of crime. In fact, if you couldn't get into a hotel, you'd just ask the taxi driver (black) to take you to a home where you could stay. Not that all blacks were well-off. There were three levels, each geared to the kind of job you had. The very poorest blacks lived from hand to mouth and didn't have regular work. If you worked on the South Side of Chicago, you worked for a black and were in the middle group. But the plum jobs in the cities were in the post office. People went to a lot of trouble to get them. One fellow I visited had set up fake pigeon holes to practice sorting mail, so he'd have a better chance of getting on at the post office. Blacks who held such jobs were considered well-off not just because of the money but because they had such benefits as health care, vacation time, pensions, and security.

Working in the downtown hotels was lucrative, too. In fact, some blacks *paid* to work in places like the Drake and other fine hotels and clubs—just for the tips.

Many blacks thought our family was well-off because we had the money to travel. Actually, we worked extra hard so we could. Not that there was a lot of competitiveness or resentment or class distinctions. If you'd been in jail, no one held that against you because they were "survival" crimes, many times committed by naive blacks who weren't used to the big city.

Going South

We didn't go to the Deep South until after the civil rights movement had played itself through. When we did, people treated us so well it was hard to believe it had ever been otherwise. They'd call you "honey," "doll," "dear," and "mister" all the time. It never seemed forced. I felt it was done with affection. After all, most southern whites played with blacks during childhood and no doubt really cared for them. So when the rules of society changed, they could express their real feelings. Perhaps these were feelings they didn't even know they had.

I had a lot of other surprises, too, but one of the strangest was on the elevator near the front door of the Roosevelt Hotel in New Orleans. I heard someone behind me drawl in a booming voice, "It sho' is a nice day out there. I'm gonna go out and play me some golf." I assumed this was a southern white gentleman. I thought he'd be a big, round-bellied guy with rosy cheeks. I was kind of smiling to myself, thinking how funny it was that white southerners sound so much like black folks. As I got off the elevator, I glanced over my shoulder at him, and there stood a small Oriental man. That just shows, you don't have to be white to think in stereotypes.

Redd Foxx once said that it was southerners who taught blacks to use poor grammar. After all, slaves spoke African languages when they were brought here. They learned English from the poor whites and the field bosses who supervised them. There are other factors that may have influenced the speech habits of slaves, too. I read once that there are no r's in African languages, so it's no wonder that blacks would say "bod" for board and "pok" for pork.

Farther Away Places

As the children grew older and were easier to travel with, we began taking trips to locations a little farther afield during the warm months. In July, a group of us would just naturally converge in Idlewild, Michigan. There was a black summer resort there where families would get together, and it was literally like one big happy family. You knew they loved your kids, and certainly you loved theirs. Ev and I would drive with our family to Milwaukee and then catch the auto ferry to Idlewild. It was always fun to watch the process of loading and unloading cars and luggage and to have your own private cabins. The lakeside cabins where we stayed would be called time-shares today.

July was the time for all the big black entertainers to come to the Black Catskills, what they called that part of the country. It was a different feeling, especially for us. There were no class distinctions; if you could afford to be there you were accepted. We had the greatest black entertainment available at the time: Moms Mabley, Sammy Davis, Jr., the Drifters, the Four Tops, and Red Saunders and his band.

Some families we'd vacation with were from professional fields like teaching and medicine but nevertheless could just barely afford it—as was the case with us. Others were bankers, newspaper people, etc., who bought or rented cabins on the lake. We were black bourgeoisie—we owned properties and had enough income to travel. Our trips were our reward for working hard all year. We lived frugally and then enjoyed ourselves. It wasn't until we got into all the businesses that we had the extra money to go on trips. I'd leave the best employees in charge and give them a bonus. Sometimes, when we were really having a good year, we'd

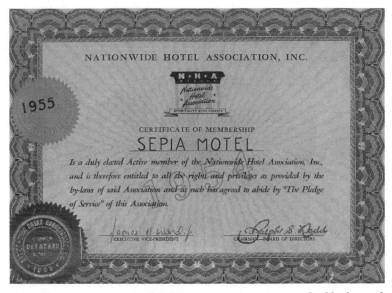

NATIONWIDE HOTEL ASSOCIATION, INC.

N · H · A
Nationwide
Hotel
Association

1955

CERTIFICATE OF MEMBERSHIP
SEPIA MOTEL

Is a duly elected Active member of the Nationwide Hotel Association, Inc.,
and is therefore entitled to all the rights and privileges as provided by the
by-laws of said Association and as such has agreed to abide by "The Pledge
of Service" of this Association.

_____
EXECUTIVE VICE-PRESIDENT

_____
CHAIRMAN—BOARD OF DIRECTORS

*Traveling cross-country in the 1950s was no easy matter for blacks, so I
started my own motel where anyone could stay regardless of color, religion, or whatever. This certificate shows that the Sepia Motel was a member of the Nationwide Hotel Association, which had its own guidebook for
blacks. It listed some friendly white motels. In Cedar Rapids, one was
Dutch Winegar's Twin Towers.*

close down for a month with pay and bonuses so we could all go
on vacation.

In Sepia

In our part of the country there were few places to accommo-
date black travelers. So in 1954 we built a motel on the corner of
our property in Cedar Rapids called the Sepia. We wanted it to
be a place where anyone could stay . . . white or black. It would
be such a good motel everyone would want to stay there. And by
golly, they did. We hosted rich and poor, black and white.

It took seven months to get it licensed because the county commission said we were out of compliance. I finally called a local
factory owner who had clout and was a friend of mine. The next
day I received my permit to open.

CECIL REED and his wife, Evelyn, prepare to address notices that lo... and perhaps the Midwest's only motel for the exclusive accommodation of ...groes is open east of Cedar Rapids on highway 30. Known as "The Sepia" motel building now has four sleeping units, two bath-and-toilet units. Surr... ing areas will be developed to give outdoor cooking and picnic facili...

SHADIEST SPOT IN IOWA

MOTEL SEPIA

Year-Round Accommodations · Showers · Forced Air Heat

On Coast-to-Coast Highway 30, 3 miles east of
CEDAR RAPIDS, IOWA

Phone 3-8881   MRS. EVELYN REED, Prop

This picture of Ev and me appeared in the Cedar Rapids Gazette *when we opened the Sepia Motel in 1953. Although the cutline stated that it was "perhaps the Midwest's only motel for the exclusive accommodation of Negroes," that's not what we intended and that's not how it worked out. Whites and blacks stayed there. The picture shows us sending out announcements (below).*

The Sepia turned out to be one of the Reeds' most satisfying and successful enterprises. It was on the Lincoln Highway and put us in touch with all kinds of people from all over the country. About five years later they moved the highway. But since each cabin had a bath, a kitchenette, and a sitting area, we converted them into rental units. It actually worked out better because they were easy to rent and didn't require so much daily attention.

Our travels, the success of the Sepia Motel, and the progress of the civil rights movement really raised my hopes and ambitions to move as freely in the rest of the world as I now could in Cedar Rapids. We'd never been West; the time seemed right. Carol was sixteen, Dick was twelve, Mike was seven, and Davey was three. Ev and I felt they should see a little of the land to the west of us, and we wanted to see some of it ourselves. So we planned a trip that would ultimately take us on a loop via the northern route to California through Utah and Oregon, then home by way of Arizona, New Mexico, and Texas.

Although by this time the Public Accommodation Act had been passed, guaranteeing equal hotel and restaurant service to all, I knew that a law doesn't change the heart and that we'd need some careful planning to avoid trouble. Having been born into this way of life, I was not too concerned by the problems I knew would confront us. But I did worry for my children. I didn't want to show hatred or fear. I didn't want them to grow up resenting and hating the world they lived in . . . nor did I want them to think their parents were "Uncle Toms." So we tried to prepare them one step at a time for the world outside Cedar Rapids where the Reeds were already established and accepted. Besides, this was uncharted territory. We had no network of "cottages," familiar people, or black hotels to contact along the way.

Westward Ho

We left on a bright August morning in 1955. The station wagon was loaded with clothes, sandwiches, and a cooler full of Kool Aid. We got an early start across Iowa. There was a gentle breeze blowing, and the corn seemed to wave and bow to us as if to help us on our way.

When we got to Nebraska, we stopped to visit Boys Town. I told the fellow in charge about the old haunted house and the priest who'd hired us to pass out fliers. The guide went into his office and came out with an old picture of that same priest standing in front of the haunted house. He said, "Cecil, the priest who hired you was Father Flanagan."

We couldn't stop at hotels in Omaha, and so we went on to Lincoln. I talked to a black man there who told me about a black church that was having a dinner that night. So we stopped for a good hearty meal, then drove on.

This part of the trip was difficult. For long periods I'd drive all night and day with my eyes burning and my muscles aching, sometimes pulling off on a side road to get a few hours' sleep. It was uncharted territory for us. We would eat in restaurants along the way that would have us, but we never knew for sure which ones would accept us. Occasionally, there would be an AAA motel about full that would keep us for the night. You can see that it was not a very relaxed trip.

Denver was an exception. It had a thriving black community in the Five Points area. We stopped there for several days and stayed at the Renaissance Hotel. There were restaurants, nightclubs, and hotels for blacks. And on Sunday we went to a beautiful Catholic church. It wasn't a black church, but we were at ease there. We found that to be true throughout the trip; wherever we were, we were always welcome in a Catholic church.

We left Denver about noon and drove all day and all night to Salt Lake City. I was exhausted and worried. On the way in, we'd seen a wreck. A truck had lost its brakes and run into a reservoir. There seemed to be hundreds of lights flashing all around us. As we came down that long road into the city, I felt dread and fear of what might happen. Everyone in the car was asleep, and I wondered if I'd be able to protect them from the physical and emotional dangers ahead.

Mormon Surprise

I drove around Salt Lake City not knowing where to go or what to do until I came to Chapel Square, that beautiful compound where the Mormon church is headquartered and where a Mormon-owned hotel is located. I told the fellow at the gate that I needed a place for my family. To my great relief and surprise, he welcomed us. He fixed us up with hotel and restaurant accommodations and told us about points of interest in the area. So we stayed a while and got a good look at Salt Lake City.

We'd always heard that Mormons didn't like blacks, but our experience was different. Because we were so well received in the next towns we visited, I suspect that the Mormons in Salt Lake called ahead to their friends in Moab, Provo, and Mission Valley. There were no other blacks to be seen, but everyone was genuinely warm and friendly.

We'd heard that Paradise Valley on the outskirts of Provo was a beautiful and unusual place. And it was. To get there, you drove through a canyon with huge rock formations on both sides. One of them was especially inspiring. It looked like a mysterious hand had carved a gigantic statue of the Virgin Mary. We drove and drove up that canyon until finally we came to a hotel where the canyon ended. It was rightly named the Deadend Hotel. It was like a world unto itself. We were so intrigued, we stayed several days. When we left, the college kids who worked there sang, "So long, it's been good to know you," and sent us on our way with a warm feeling.

Moab was the most interesting of these stops. It was a busy, booming town and had been, I guess, ever since uranium was discovered there. Mining activities were at peak levels. We stayed at the Tuxedo Hotel, where the lady who ran it saw to it that we went to the best and most hospitable restaurants. We had such a good time that on our return trip we drove out of our way to stop there again. We left Mike's bag there, but by the time we got home, the hotel manager had mailed it to us at her own expense.

A Gamble in Nevada

Next we went to Sparks, Nevada, a little tourist oasis in the middle of the desert. The AAA had scheduled us into a motel there, but we couldn't reach it until the middle of the night. Since the lodging was prepaid, the owner simply left a key for us with a note telling us where our rooms were and where to drop the key if we left early. The next morning, I got up about five and was walking around. The woman who was at the desk said, "My God, what are *you* doing here." I laughed and told her I was the one with reservations who came in late. There was no problem, just a little shock. In fact, the owner took me around Needles to show me the town and even introduced me to his banker.

There were some other touchy moments in Nevada. As we were leaving the state, we stopped at a counter restaurant, and I went in to check the lay of the land. The manager said, "Mister, I can't serve you here, but if you'll move to the back counter, I can." Then he whispered in a confidential way, "Crossing from Nevada into California—it'll be like going into heaven for you folks. Everything is wide open there." I knew what he meant.

We didn't stop in Sacramento, but we could tell when we were in the black part of town by the music. It was a beautiful section but still had a different feel about it. The differences were even more pronounced in San Francisco. The white area was very formal, while the black section, on Fillmore Street, was noisy and comfortable. But no one gave you a second look wherever you were in San Francisco or whatever your color. I guess it was because there was such a mixture of people, cultures, and ideas. Differences were accepted, if they were noticed at all.

Initially, we stayed at an AAA hotel, the Raphael, that was first-class. In fact, it was so fancy the help wore tuxedos. It was a nice experience, but we wanted to be more relaxed, and I wanted the kids to see the black area. So after a few days we moved to Fillmore Street, which had its own first-class black hotels and restaurants. The Russian district was nearby, and my Czech language skills broke down the barriers there.

Southern California

After San Francisco, we headed south to Los Angeles and the Watkins Hotel off Central Avenue near Adams. We were there a week and saw a lot of show business blacks. At that time, the area was filled with beautiful restaurants, black-owned grocery stores, insurance companies, etc.

We took the kids to the La Brea Tar Pits. They were really excited to see the dinosaur bones and the tar bubbling up right there in the middle of the city. It was an awesome thought that the same forces were still at work that had trapped those dinosaurs millions of years ago. We heard that the only other place where they are so close to the surface is at Haiti's asphalt lakes. I doubt they have any dinosaur bones there, but they've been paving their streets with that asphalt for a hundred years. I've heard that the Haitians even put asphalt over their graves, which are sometimes under their streets. I was told that some who believe in voodoo do this to avoid having their dead loved ones dug up and turned into zombies.

We went to the usual tourist spots but had a better than usual time. After Knotts Berry Farm we went to Disneyland. It was opening day and wasn't quite completed. As we walked in, the greeter said: "This is your lucky day. You are the one thousandth family to visit Disneyland, and you get the day free."

Next, we drove south to San Diego where we stopped at the Fergusons, who were relatives of Jack and Betty West, our neighbors in Cedar Rapids. The Fergusons lived in a very nice area, El Cajon. During the week we were there, we all took a bus to Mexico and saw a bullfight—all but Mrs. Ferguson, who couldn't bear to watch it.

We had an exciting taxi ride out to the bullfight arena. The streets were dusty and narrow, and we went careening around corners and down alleyways. People would leap out of the way at the last minute. No one was directing traffic. Our cabdriver shrugged and said, "Oh, them crazy Mexican cabdrivers." As we started home, we stopped for dinner. We noticed that one guy was eating black meat. We wondered what it was. He asked if we had watched the bull fights and added, "That's the bull."

Grand Canyon

When we left San Diego, we came back east by way of Grand Canyon. We camped in the national park on both of the canyon's beautiful rims. Early in the morning there'd be lots of deer that would come right up to you. From the observation areas, the people riding the burros down in the canyon looked so tiny, you'd get an idea of how deep and wide it was. You had to be in awe of the power and time it took to carve the canyon. You also had to admire the hardy pioneers who settled there and even went on farther west. Then, when we saw Lake Mead and Boulder Dam, I was struck by the great energy, imagination, and ability of our modern pioneers who accomplished so much at those sites.

Across the Desert

As we drove through the desert, we traveled at high noon even though people had warned us that it would be too hot. We didn't have air-conditioned cars in those days, but I rigged up a contraption that worked pretty well. I took an air duct off a furnace and installed it in the window. This duct guided the air stream that was created by the car's movement. I laid a sponge soaked with water inside the duct which cooled the air coming into the car. It was sort of like a swamp cooler. Sometimes I'd put dry ice in the sponge, which really helped a lot. I was always careful with it, though, to make sure there was plenty of air circulating so we wouldn't have trouble with the fumes from the dry ice. This system worked so well I used it on my trucks at home.

Ev had packed a separate suitcase for each child and a little kit with paper, pencils, games, and books. Each of them had a canvas bag of water. They made up games along the way, pretending that they were lost in the desert, seeing mirages, and looking for gold. They had so much fun with their own canteens that they drank more water than they really needed, even in the desert. Then, too, we had Coolie Pops for them in a cooler. All this led to a lot of roadside stops, but at least nobody got dehydrated.

We stopped at a filling station with a giant papier-mâché cowboy out front. It stood behind a water fountain that tourists drank from. As someone approached the station for a drink, a voice would seem to come out of the cowboy's mouth and talk to them. The owner of the filling station was a pretty big guy who was the "voice." We noticed a cup and bucket of water sitting off to the side and thought it was for blacks, so we started toward it. The voice from the cowboy said, "Don't drink that," and we thought we were in trouble. But then he said, "No, that's for Indians." It was an uncomfortable feeling to be favored over another group of people. I had to wonder what he would say if he knew I had Indian blood.

We had an eerie experience when we were approaching Bear Canyon. We were running low on gas as darkness was falling. I was getting a little nervous about where we might stay and if we'd have enough gasoline to get there. Then I noticed a light in the distance. As we drew near, I saw a gasoline station off to the side where we stopped and filled up. When we finally got past Bear Canyon, we were eating at a restaurant, and I told the waitress about our experience. She said very firmly, "There's no filling station up there."

Homeward Bound

The trip home was fast. As it came to an end, we were suddenly homesick. Also, we were eager to be in Des Moines for a big church convention two days later. So we drove night and day to get to Denver and left again the very next morning. All told, the trip was about thirty days long. We'd seen some of the most beautiful parts of our country: awesome mountains, valleys, deserts, cities, buildings, and forests. We'd seen hostility and friendship, selfishness and generosity. We'd felt fear and love. I think we all grew from the trip. I believe the trip helped the children to understand more about discrimination and to realize that they could deal with it.

You can see that our family trip West was not a cure-all for discrimination, but it was great progress in the context of our lives and times. It was only a few years earlier that Ev and I had a very different kind of experience. We took a bus trip out of our "safe" territory through Joplin, Missouri, to Albuquerque, New Mexico, and Flagstaff, Arizona. We started out with sandwiches we'd brought from home. When they ran out, the bus drivers would tell us to stay on the bus, and they would bring us sandwiches. They didn't want us to be embarrassed. We understood what they were telling us. Then, when we were in Dallas, Ev went to the bathroom and found a sign that said "whites only." She went to the black bathroom but it was dirty. By then, she was tired and disgusted with this kind of treatment, so she went to the white restroom. I guess she was just getting up a head of steam, because then she refused to sit in the black waiting room. Finally, she sat on the white side of the lunchroom. Frankly, I was getting pretty nervous about what would happen, but then a policeman came and politely escorted her back to my side. He kind of smiled and nodded.

A few months after we returned from our trip West something happened that reminded me of this bus trip and Ev's determination and bravery. On December 1, Rosa Parks, a black seamstress in Montgomery, Alabama, refused to give up her bus seat to a white man and mobilized the anger of the city's black community. Four days later, 90 percent of Montgomery's black population walked or hitchhiked to a rally organized by Dr. Martin Luther King to desegregate public transportation. And the rest is history. Sometimes I think it takes a strong woman to get these things done.

9   **A** Visit from a Nice Little Jewish Guy

The civil rights movement was on fire at the busiest time of my life, when my family and business responsibilities were heaviest. I was operating several businesses—the floor maintenance service and supply store plus the Sepia Motel. Ev and I were buying, fixing up, and selling properties. We had a growing family with all their activities to attend. We were active in community organizations, fund drives, cultural exchange programs, and school functions.

At the same time, calls were coming from all directions for me to speak. Whenever someone wanted me to go somewhere to talk about black history and civil rights, I went. There was great interest in these topics, and I seemed to be the most likely person to ask. I wasn't paid to speak; in fact, most speeches cost me money for transportation and clothing—and sometimes I bought my own meals and contributed to the group's funding. But I wanted to speak. It seemed both an opportunity and a duty that, in good conscience, I couldn't turn down.

But I was stretched to the maximum physically and emotionally, and so was my budget. Even with all the work we all did, there never seemed to be enough money. And lots of times I worried whether my busy schedule allowed me to give my family the attention they needed and deserved. When I would sit down for a few minutes, I'd wonder if it was the right thing, especially when I had so many financial responsibilities.

One night I'd had a particularly hard day working at the floor-sanding business. I came home to watch the motel till it filled because the woman who worked the desk for me couldn't make it that night. Sitting on a chair on the front porch of the motel, I leaned back and listened to the comforting sounds of a beautiful, warm Iowa evening . . . the crickets and frogs, the wind in the trees, a dog howling, and even a deer rustling through the woods beside the motel.

I was discouraged and worried. As a small businessman, every day had to be almost perfectly carried out because you had to think of making payroll, putting the workmen's compensation money in escrow, maintaining trucks and machines, and buying gas, oil, and supplies. Should I be spending what little free time I had making free speeches? What if I got sick from the pace I was keeping? Sometimes I'd go for three or four days at a time with no rest. What if the businesses failed because I was spreading myself too thin?

I don't know whether I dozed or exactly what happened, but all of a sudden I heard a boom. The light around the motel became so bright it lit up the entire surrounding area. Suddenly this little guy just appeared before me. He was about 5 feet 9 or 10 with long black hair, very kind eyes, and an athletic build. There seemed to be a light around his head. He reminded me of a man in Omaha whom all of us kids used to call Rags. Rags was a Jewish guy who made his living by collecting rags and metal in a wagon and then selling them.

My visitor said to me rather casually, "I like your sign." I thought he meant the neon sign out by the road for the motel. But he said, "No, that one," and pointed to a reflector kind of sign on the front of the building that said, "Love Thy Neighbor." I'd never seen it before and was kind of stunned. Then he looked me directly in the eye and said, "Don't worry, it will all work out. You are doing the right thing. Just keep making your speeches and doing everything you're doing, and you'll never have to worry about money again." Just like that he turned and walked away—in the direction of the house. He went away, and the light went with him. A few minutes later, Dick came over from the house to call me for supper. I asked, "Did you see that little Jewish guy who was just here?" Dick said, "I didn't see anyone. There couldn't have been anyone—the dogs didn't bark." I always wondered after that if I'd had a dream or a vision.

From that day on, a calmness came over me, and I didn't dislike anyone. I didn't worry as much. Life seemed much smoother. I had a good feeling in my heart for everyone and for this wonderful country we live in. I could see something positive in everyone and everything.

I can't describe the feeling that came over me that night, but it still comes once in a while. Sometimes when I'm resting before a speech or talking to a group or thinking after a speech, that wonderful feeling comes over me. I feel love and confidence that everything is working out. Sometimes I can still see the picture of him walking away with that light around him. I've described it to friends, who say it sounds like an aura.

I really didn't know what to think about it. I know I felt relieved of my burdens and hopeful. I did what he suggested, and you know, the money just came. Ever after that, I never did worry about money. I spend my energies doing what I feel needs to be done; I contribute money to groups and causes that seem important to me. And it brings me riches in return. Not that I'm rich or don't have to be careful with money, but since that experience my energies are always renewed, and there's always enough money to do the things that count. I've discussed this with several ministers, and now I wonder if that man who reminded me of Jesus might have been an angel. One thing I'm sure of, he came to set my mind at ease so I could continue talking to people. But I got more out of it than just peace of mind. Ever since that night, I have cared about all people. Until then, I didn't see others' pain. Now I care about every person in this beautiful flower garden of colors we call the United States. I'm concerned about every person who is hungry or homeless, sick or discouraged. This might sound like an added burden—to worry about everyone. But I also get pleasure from the successes and happiness of others. And I get love. They know I love them, and they love me in return. God bless America.

10   Quit Talking and Do It

The way things were in the early sixties, I suppose it's
not surprising that I ended up running for public office. Because
of television, the whole country saw the beatings and mistreat-
ment of civil rights demonstrators in Alabama and other states. I
think it was pretty shocking to blacks *and* whites to see such
things live on television. It's one thing to hear rumors of cross
burnings and beatings, but it's another to see a city's fire hoses
and police dogs turned on little children and grandmothers.

The Black Revolution had begun, and its presence was felt in Cedar Rapids. Ev and I had been speaking about black history for several years in the school system and later to all kinds of groups. I had talked to church and civic groups all over. Our kids were active in all kinds of church and school activities.

We had recently moved into town (to Mt. Vernon Road) so our teenagers could be more in the thick of things, and we were well known in three different areas of Cedar Rapids. The whites in this broad area were fairly comfortable with blacks . . . at least the Reed kind. As the civil rights movement gathered momentum, the community looked more and more to Ev and me for our opinions and help in understanding what was going on. In view of all this, I suppose I was a natural to run for office and win. But the idea never occurred to me until a friend suggested it in a way that was more like a dare than anything else.

A Dare or a Challenge?

Father Cassidy was the chaplain at Mercy Hospital where I had a floor maintenance contract. We became friends while we worked with various youth groups. He'd go to business meetings, young married groups, etc., with me to learn about their problems. In turn, he introduced me to the world of Catholicism. I was inspired by the devotion of the priests and nuns I met and truly enjoyed their company.

I used to help them put on a dance and show to raise money for the nursing schools. One of the nuns told me about Martín de Porres, the seventeenth-century Afro-Spanish saint who was so gentle that small animals followed him wherever he went. It was said that whenever you prayed to him and it was to be answered, a small animal would appear. One winter day, I was to take four sisters to an important meeting in Waukon. The weather had turned bad, and the radio repeatedly cautioned listeners about the hazardous driving conditions. When we got into the nuns' station wagon, one sister asked that we pray to St. de Porres for a safe trip. When we finished praying, a mouse ran up the outside of her sleeve! She brushed it off out the window, and we drove away. Although the roads were covered with ice, we didn't slip even once all the way up and back.

Father Cassidy and I used to talk about how to change things and people, how to solve community problems. I kind of built up a network with priests and nuns. A priest in another parish might call me up and say, "I've got a black guy who needs a job. What can we do to help him?" And I'd usually be able to come up with something. I was always off on one track or another. Finally, one day Father Cassidy said to me: "Why don't you quit talking and do it. We all agree with you, but you have to get it done. Get yourself elected to the state legislature so you can do something about all these ideas you have."

Well, that felt like a challenge. And the fact that he felt I could win an election and do the job seemed like a vote of confidence. So I talked it over with Ev, and we were on our way. I was an especially acceptable candidate because I was a Republican in a largely Republican area. Also, I always "braced the system" before I made any moves so that whites wouldn't feel threatened by me or my family.

It was 1966 and I was running for the Iowa State General Assembly as a Republican against a labor leader. Today, people are surprised that I ran on the Republican ticket. What they don't realize is that most blacks of my parents' generation felt an allegiance to Abraham Lincoln, a Republican, for "freeing the slaves." I took on the political beliefs of my parents and the white farmers and small businessowners we knew. It was not until Franklin Roosevelt's presidency that most blacks became Democrats. He forged an alliance among minorities, poor people, union members, and longtime Democrats.

I had no money or campaign experience, but I did have a core group of helpers comprised of a dozen schoolchildren, my family, and five special friends, John Ely, Bud Jensen, Thomas Riley, Howard Hall, and Joan Lipsky. As we began work on the campaign, I realized that I *really* wanted to serve in the state legislature. I felt sure I could solve some of the problems because I understood them and cared deeply about finding solutions.

Soon, there were others helping us. I'd gotten to know another

WHEN THE REEDS BOUGHT this home on 15 acres of land just off the old highway to Mount Vernon some of the neighbors at first objected. Later the same neighbors became good friends. At one time Reed donated some land for use as a small park and, with the neighbors' help, provided it with picnic facilities and recreational equipment.

This is the campaign photo we used when I ran for office. It shows, left to right, Carol, Dick, Davey, Evelyn, me, Mike, and our dog, Rocket. The house shown was located just off the old highway to Mount Vernon, but we had moved into town (also on Mount Vernon Road) by the time the campaign was under way. Des Moines Register *photo by Joan Liffring.*

priest, Father Stemm, from working each year on a fund-raiser that featured Don Ameche, the film star. He went to school in Dubuque under Father Stemm and so admired him that he sent his two sons to school in Cedar Rapids. Don used to come in to help raise money for Father Stemm's church, All Saints.

Kid Campaign

There probably haven't been many campaigns like mine. I was not a politician. In fact, I'd never attended a party caucus until I ran for office. Most of my campaigners were kids. That happened soon after we got started. My signs disappeared from the lawns of my supporters. We were trying to figure out what had happened to them. Well, the mystery was solved when I was invited to school to talk to a civics class. When I walked in, the missing signs were posted all over the room. The students wanted to surprise me. Many of them knew me from playing in Lincoln Park. They'd watched the midget car races we used to have and the ball games we used to play. They'd decided to play a little trick on me by gathering all my signs into the classroom. So I said to them, "If you're going to steal my signs, you'd better help me get elected." And they did.

One kid's dad owned a printing company. He took a roll of sandpaper that cost me $50 and made cards that said:

ROUGH AIN'T IT?

WANT A CHANGE?

VOTE FOR CECE REED

Another boy's father owned an insurance company and did our computer work. One girl's dad owned a car rental agency, so we had plenty of transportation.

They were all a wonderful help to me, and I think it was good for them, too. One girl got so interested in politics she became a page in the state legislature. She also learned to drive because of it. She was a page while I was serving there but still living in Cedar Rapids. When I'd come home on weekends, I'd give her a ride home. Many times I was so exhausted, I'd let her drive. You can imagine my surprise when her father called me later to thank me for teaching her to drive. I didn't have the heart to tell him that I thought she already knew how and that I had slept through most of her driving.

A better-known campaign helper was Richard Nixon. He came through Cedar Rapids, and I had my picture taken with him at the airport. Others said he was cold and remote, but he seemed warm to me. While I can't condone everything that happened at Watergate, I appreciate his accomplishments. He did more for black people in government than any other president in my lifetime. He appointed blacks to key positions where real progress could be made. And they weren't token jobs—you didn't get appointed unless you were really qualified. Ev and I were invited to Nixon's inaugural, but family matters kept us from going.

When the votes were in, Cecil Reed was the second-highest vote getter in Linn County. My opponent, Allen Meier, was a nice fellow, but the timing was right for me to win. Apparently he

When I was running for the state legislature in 1966, Richard Nixon was making a comeback after unsuccessful campaigns for president and then governor of California. He came to Cedar Rapids on a Republican fund-raising trip. The then-mayor of Cedar Rapids, Robert Johnson, is on the left. He later followed in my footsteps and became a state legislator. In the background is Joan Lipsky, also of Linn County, who was elected to the state legislature the same year I was.

didn't hold it against me because recently, as labor commissioner for the state of Iowa, he signed off on a move to name the state law library in the Department of Labor after me.

The people had spoken, and the candidate and his campaigners were very happy. Two television stations called us in, and we went there with Joan Lipsky, a successful candidate herself, and then on to an election-night party. I think the Iowa voters in the Cedar Rapids area were really stretching themselves to be open-minded in that election. The four legislators they elected were truly varied: a black entrepreneur; Joan Lipsky, who was Jewish; Nathan "Fritz" Sorg, a pharmacist; and Scott McIntyre, an insurance man who was disabled.

The Sweet Sorrow of Leaving

The years in Cedar Rapids had been well spent. Evelyn and I were given many awards. The mayor presented me with the flag of Cedar Rapids. It had been given to only six other people, and so I prize it highly. The local newspaper, the *Cedar Rapids Gazette*, gave me an award for "outstanding service to the community." The city council made me an honorary Cedar Rapidian. When the *Des Moines Register* reported this award they said, "Probably few men have ever been named honorary residents of cities where they have lived for four decades."

I appreciated all the awards and honors, but I knew that I was still plain old Cecil Reed just trying to fit in. It was brought home to me one night very clearly that discrimination was not over for me or other blacks. Ev and I were going out to dinner with another couple to celebrate my birthday. She was waiting in the car for me to drive over and pick them up. Two policemen came by and asked for me. It turned out that one of my trucks had several parking tickets which I didn't know about because an employee had failed to mention them to me. But my name and address were on the title, so a warrant was out for my arrest. I explained the situation to the officers, and they could see that I was a responsible citizen by the way I was dressed and where I lived. But when they called the office for instructions, I heard a voice say,

"Bring the nigger in." They seemed embarrassed but took me to police headquarters. I don't think this would have happened to a white person—especially one who had a long-standing business and was a candidate for public office. To this day I don't know whose voice that was. I'm sure he thought no one but the policemen would hear it. I know it's hard to change habits, but when you're a civil servant, you're setting an example for others. I was released quickly, and we went on with our dinner, but it left me feeling sad. Luckily, the good people of Cedar Rapids elected me to office in a landslide vote a few weeks later.

I brushed this hurt aside because there were so many honors and reluctant good-byes from the people who really knew me. I reminded myself and my family that we had to *buy* a house to live in because no one in Cedar Rapids would rent to us at the time, but when we left, our neighbors told us they nearly got up a petition to keep us from leaving. It felt good to have changed so many minds and made such inroads. But I also knew that my children had suffered taunts and rejection as part of this progress. What they went through was much less than I had experienced as a child, but watching it happen to them, especially to Davey, the youngest and tenderest, hurt me much more.

But all of them helped me put the Reeds in a good light in Cedar Rapids. When the opportunity to run for office came my way, the Reed family reputation was a real plus. We were all on our way to a new life. For me, it was the end of my life in the private sector. It was the end of being an entrepreneur and the beginning of being a public servant. I didn't think much about it at the time—I was too busy. But in retrospect, I believe that it was a natural step for me to take. I've not regretted it because I firmly believe that serving the public is an honorable and important thing to do.

For all of us, it was a shift from being prominent blacks in a small town to being very visible blacks in a much larger setting. But we remained flies in the buttermilk. And I was to become highly visible in the short time I served in the legislature.

11   **A** Long Six Months

I was one of six newly elected Republicans to be sworn in to the Sixty-seventh General Assembly, state of Iowa, in a dignified ceremony on January 9, 1967. I was extremely moved and impressed by the occasion. *I* impressed all those present, but not in a way I would have chosen.

The House of Representatives in the state of Iowa meets in a beautiful, ornate chamber designed in much the same way as the English House of Lords. The arched tiers of mahogany desks, the graceful balustrades, and the red velvet seats create a majestic atmosphere that makes you realize what an important responsibility the voters have entrusted you with. I felt both honored and nervous.

The chaplain opened with an earnest prayer. The Speaker of the House invited the six new members to come to the speaker's platform in the well of the House for the swearing in. He administered the oath of office in his authoritative baritone voice, and we all solemnly responded in unison. As we returned to our seats, Cecil Reed, the only black in the group, fell up the steps! I was wearing my new (and first) bifocals. No one laughed, but I felt terrible. I was off to a stumbling start!

Busier Than Ever

The years leading up to my election had been busy ones, and the campaign itself was a whirlwind of activity and excitement, but the six months that followed were the most frantic, exhausting ones of my life. They were also the most exhilarating and satisfying because of the things I learned, the people I met, and the important duties I was entrusted with.

I literally worked night and day during those six months. Even as I slept, my mind was puzzling out ways to do what I knew needed to be done. I knew the time was right to make a difference in the lives of many people. I was driven by the feeling that I had an opportunity I'd never really thought would come my way . . . and I couldn't be sure I'd ever get another chance.

My first impression of the legislature was surprise at how polite everyone was. The language was formal and couched in the most genteel form: "Would the gentleman from so and so county be so kind as to yield two minutes of your time to your worthy colleague." "The gentleman from Linn County has the floor." While a lot of this was pure ceremony, I found that this tradition served a valuable purpose: to keep behavior civil. Behaving like ladies and gentlemen helps you express yourself thoughtfully and intelligently. Conducting business in a rational language teaches you how to solve problems in a positive way.

In the legislature, this polite behavior carried over even when you weren't in session. Occasionally, people would lose their tempers, but they'd never lose control totally. Considering how emotional most of the legislature's business is, the members' civilized behavior was pretty remarkable. I think it makes a valid case for using good manners in personal relationships and everyday dealings. You might be at each other's throat, but maintaining the decorum keeps rancor at a low level and allows you to get the job done. I found, too, that this civilized attitude prevailed on both sides of the aisle and that, if your intentions were honest, even your opponents would give you a helping hand.

I already knew the importance of compromise, but the legislature's decorum taught me the art of achieving it. Compromise and polite behavior are the oil that keep our House and Senate running smoothly. You can't get things done there without the cooperation of others. You must get sponsors for your bills, and you must win the support of many legislators. You must have some way of persuading your colleagues that your cause is just or practical or in their best interest—or all of the above. You must figure out what appeal it has to the person you are trying to get on board.

There is back scratching: "I'll do this if you do that." And some horse trading. This might seem shady, but it is a system that works because of the underlying politeness. If intentions are good, it works for the best. Even if they're not, it still can work. If you keep your integrity, you'll get the most you can for your constituency.

Usually, you don't get all you want, but you do get started. Keep in mind that the other person has to win sometimes, and there's always the chance that you aren't totally right. This approach keeps a check and balance on your own spirit, which can sometimes carry you off in the wrong direction.

While the legislature operates on compromise, that did not include compromising principles, at least not for me. I never stayed with any committee or issue I didn't believe in. Once on a committee proposing to install rest stops on a freeway, I signed on because it sounded like a good thing for travelers. Later, I realized that the group the lobbyist represented would profit way out of proportion to the public good that would be served. At my request, I was released from the sponsorship.

Learning the Ropes

In a short time, I learned a lot about how the legislative process works—both in theory and in practice. And I learned it from other people. I found that when you're in a situation where you don't know the ropes and you need to learn them in a hurry, the best thing to do is to turn to those who do.

I learned the importance of having an experienced secretary who could tell you where everyone stood and what to watch out for. Sandy Yizer was my secretary. Even though she was a rookie, too, she had tremendous technical skills and a special ability to figure out how to get things done. Maybe it was because she was a minister's wife who knew how to network. She reached out to others to help them and for help. She had a knack for putting a bill together and for finding the procedures to follow in getting it before the floor and through the voting process. She also taught me the protocol of working with other legislators and their staffs.

Besides Sandy, people in the Legislative Service Bureau (lawyers and secretaries) helped me observe the congressional intent of the laws that passed. Sometimes language is put in legislation to evade points that are hidden to the layperson. The research people would analyze the language, point out the underlying meaning, and thereby help me avoid supporting a point I did not believe in.

I also learned from people who opposed me. I learned to carefully analyze all sides of an issue and to make sure I understood everyone's point of view. It's like tournament debaters. They don't know which side they'll be debating and so must prepare arguments for both sides. Thinking through other points of view helps you understand your own better and enables you to present your own opinion with deeper conviction.

The legislative secretaries were whizzes at organizing the bills and using the correct language, and they were most generous in sharing their knowledge and time with a fledgling legislator. When Sandy was sick, others would help, even if they were with the opposing party. I believe they were committed to serving the public as best they could, and they saw that I sincerely wanted to learn.

Listening

In working with all these people, I followed Father Cassidy's wisdom when he said, "Listening is a sacrament." I found if I listened to lobbyists—both sides—I could get a good education. Lobbyists know what they're talking about. They have the statistics on everything imaginable. I listened to these experts from both sides and then made my decision. What a wonderful, quick way to get educated on a topic.

But I also went outside the legislative setting when preparing to make decisions about issues and bills. I'd talk to the League of Women Voters who do thorough research on current topics. I'd go to the Welfare Association in the state. They knew about bills having to do with social legislation and could give me sound pro and con arguments on them. The Migrants' Action Committee was another valuable resource for information. I was on the committee's board in Iowa. Professional and manufacturers' associations as well as unions were invaluable sources of information and support. For example, I found that the builders' association, both state and national, electrical contractors, cement contractors, and trade unions were quite useful in gathering information about highway issues.

There were no black lobbyists per se. Of course, people from the Urban League and the NAACP would stay in touch and let me know how they felt about specific issues. But many times I'd turn to former black legislators, even though they were Democrats. I particularly remember Wilma Glanton, wife of Judge Glanton, who was always helpful. Another was James Walker, a very sharp lawyer who was hired out of the legislature by the Pepsi Cola company. He could give me the legal point of view on most anything.

I found that the students in university law schools would conduct research for you. It was necessary to check all the details in a bill since every little word and punctuation mark could affect the meaning of a sentence. These soon-to-be lawyers were good at editing such details. Students and professors in schools of commerce would help you with budget and economic matters.

One of the best sources of information was the Chambers of

Commerce in various towns and cities. They'd analyze all the bills in the hopper. They'd send you a whole packet with a clear and careful analysis of the impact that the bills would have on their communities. It always amazed me how one change—for example, the opening or closing of a street or highway—could affect a whole community.

Multiple Issues

I was determined not to be a one-issue legislator. That could easily have happened since I was the first black Republican elected to the Iowa House of Representatives, and there was only one other black there, a Democrat named June Franklin. Because of the times and my unique situation, I'm sure people thought I'd focus on civil rights issues exclusively. But I'd been an entrepreneur, homeowner, family man, and taxpayer too long not to have broad interests in how the government worked. I just wanted to represent my whole constituency. Therefore, I plunged into studying and developing bills on topics related to my other main concerns: vocational education, highway safety, and housing.

The House leaders put you on committees you might have expertise or interest in. So they placed me on four committees: Conservation, Industrial and Human Relations, Roads and Highways, and State Planning and Development. I was a ranking member on the Conservation Committee and as such was the spokesperson on behalf of the Republican party on conservation issues. Conservation was popular at that time, as it almost always is. Although it was not my strongest interest, the experience of talking to the press and public about conservation was very helpful in preparing me to discuss issues closer to my heart . . . housing, education, and highways.

Voting

I can't remember my first vote, but the most important early vote I participated in was a highway bill that was in committee. The highway between Cedar Rapids and Iowa City was very curvy and the site of many deaths. One of the planks in my campaign platform was to do something about that terrible death trap. It was very rewarding to be able to keep that promise during my first few weeks in office.

Working on another highway bill, building a new four-lane highway to run along the old Lincoln Highway, was a real learning experience. We wanted Illinois legislators to do the same thing so that it would be a continuous good highway across the nation, but it was not a priority for them. At that time, various states were bidding on a federal contract to build an atomic energy project. Iowa and Illinois were still in the running, but Iowa was nineteenth while Illinois was number one. I suggested to the press that Iowa should be moved ahead of Illinois because we had passed a fair housing bill in Iowa and were thus in compliance with federal requirements while they were not. Well, right away I began to hear from Illinois Senator Everett Dirksen's office. I told them we'd passed a fair housing bill in Iowa. Suddenly, they became conciliatory over the highway. One of his staff said, "You *know* you're not going to get the energy contract, but it *would* be good for the country to connect these two highways." So they did, and they passed a fair housing bill. The constituents of Iowa and Illinois were well served.

Another highway bill I sponsored never got out of committee. The idea started when I read that doctors said that getting help the first few minutes after an accident is essential if victims are to survive. Then I read that many military helicopters have complete emergency units aboard, and I wondered why they couldn't be used to quickly reach victims of highway accidents.

I proposed a plan that would divide Iowa into six quadrants, each with at least one hospital. The medical helicopters would be no more than six minutes from the quadrant hospital. And we'd use the big helicopters to remove wreckage (another safety factor). The existing highway patrol equipment and personnel could be used for communication. Newspapers wrote about my idea, and the telephone company came to me and said they'd install digital public phones for emergency use. I also learned that the army surplus would sell helicopters cheap. In spite of such support, I could never get it out of committee. Later, I was contacted by George Mills, a historian and newspaper reporter, who also thought it was a great idea. He called and said, "Another state wants a copy of your proposal." Eventually, that state received funding for a demonstration project from the federal government, and the concept is used nationwide today (except for removing wreckage). I felt sad that I couldn't make it work in my state, but I'm gratified it did happen later. Sometimes I wonder where some of my ideas came from and how I had the nerve to try to implement them.

Tech Schools

I also felt strongly that we needed to offer high school students other alternatives for higher education than the academic track. I'd been very impressed by the ideas of the renowned vocational educator, S. C. Sonickson, who said in 1932, "85 percent of all young high school and college students studied for professions while only 20 percent of the jobs required bachelor degrees. . . . We are building an imbalanced society that will bring about unrest, poverty, and vice."

According to current statistics, 85 percent are still training for the professions and we do, indeed, have unrest, poverty, and vice. I believe in higher education, but we've got to provide opportunities for all kinds of talents. The point is, we have too many professionals and not enough people to work with their hands. It reminds me of the story of the lawyer who called the plumber to fix a broken pipe. When presented with the bill, the lawyer was outraged and said, "Good lord, man, I don't make that much per hour, and I'm an attorney." The plumber replied, "Neither did I when I was a lawyer."

One of the facts I used to help sell a technical education program in Iowa was to let folks know that in many states, the only place you can learn alteration tailoring and multicolored printing is in the state reformatories. It made sense to voters to provide this kind of training out in the community, so that young people didn't have to go to jail to get it.

Ultimately, my colleagues and I came up with a program that provided for thirteen technical schools in the state, but not without a lot of study and hard work. First, we studied a state that already had some programs in place. Then we worked on a feasibility study and drummed up support. But I guess the greatest challenge was in getting all thirteen counties to work together. All the effort paid off in the end, though. Each of the counties was able to pass a mil levy to keep the schools in operation, with some aid from the state. I'm proud to say that those schools are still going today and growing by leaps and bounds.

When I introduced this bill in the House, the *Cedar Rapids Gazette* printed my description of the plan verbatim. I described what the schools would do for industry. I explained that voc tech schools were not just for kids but to train elderly workers and help them find work, too. Voc tech schools would retrain people who were employed in fields that were in decline. These schools would be tailored to people, not people to the school. Students could work at their own pace and would train in fields where jobs were developing instead of declining.

I wrote articles on the need for technical training and the design of voc tech schools for educational journals. I began to get requests from groups all over the country, some of which I still speak to today.

Black History

Another project I worked on ended up being a joint resolution of both Houses rather than a bill. It had to do with getting black history studies in the state school system. There was controversy all over the country about making black history part of the college curriculum. Ev and I had been studying black history for a long time, so I felt strongly that it should be included. As I studied Chinese history and others around the world, I realized how little was said about African history, the story of blacks. All I knew about Africa was that it was called the Dark Continent. As I researched it, I found that when we were brought to this country as slaves, many of us were from royal African families and many of us had knowledge and abilities far beyond our white masters. I heard one man speak to the Cedar Rapids Chamber of Commerce who had explored Africa and South America. The speaker, John Goddard, was an English medical doctor and pilot who toured the

United States telling about his experiences. He said that African navigators had found an oceanic river between the two continents that carried them to South America long before Columbus arrived in the Western Hemisphere. Goddard had found the remains of whole tribes of Africans in South America, complete with spears made of a gold alloy, a process unknown in Europe at that time. This helps dispel the notion that we were all half-naked illiterates running around in the jungle.

Learning all these things about my predecessors made me feel better about being black. I wanted young blacks to be reprogrammed as well (and whites with them), so that we could respect ourselves and get the respect we deserved. I'd heard an educator talk about Hitler's attempt to wipe out Jewish history because he wanted to destroy them. Hitler knew that a culture's history is vital to its survival and prosperity. By not including black history in Ancient, Medieval, World, and American history, white people did that to blacks, whether by design or by accident.

But when I proposed writing a bill to make black studies part of the state's school system, the experienced legislators advised me there was a better way of doing it. They suggested that I get a consensus for a concurrent resolution in both Houses. Their advice was good psychology. We got immediate support from school administrators. But then they said, "We don't know how to teach black history." Governor Hughes called me in and said, "Get over there and show them." He was nice about it, but I took that as an order. I was a little concerned because here I was trying to teach teachers and administrators. I'd done a lot of speechmaking but didn't really know how to teach. So I decided I'd need to do something different to get them excited about the topic first, and then maybe I could get them to do the work. And that's just what happened.

I started off with a picture exhibit that showed some of the contributions blacks had made around the world and particularly in this country. I showed pictures of famous white people who'd had gifted black assistants: Thomas Edison with Louis Lattimore, who made the incandescent element for the light bulb that gave it the ability to be turned off and on. Dr. Jonas Salk with Adam Wade, a black biochemist and medical technician who was also

This is part of the exhibit I made for the black history class I taught to schoolteachers and administrators at Governor Harold Hughes's request. It later was used in many classes, conferences, and meetings, as shown in this picture from the Kansas City, Missouri, weekly newspaper, The Call, *in November 1969. I'm explaining the poster to my boss at that time, William S. Harris, Regional Manpower administrator.*

an entertainer and athlete. He had a TV show in Los Angeles and made several gold records. Alexander Graham Bell with G. T. Wood, a black engineer who designed air brakes and sold the rights to Westinghouse. He also invented station-to-station telegraph service and another service that enabled communication between moving trains. He drew one of the first diagrams of the telephone.

Others shown in the exhibit included a black Georgia railroad worker, Andrew Byrd, who invented an automatic coupling device for joining boxcars; a number of important black Catholics, including saints; African blacks who were emperors, scientists, engineers, teachers, and artisans; Cheops, who built the great pyramid; the lost tribes of Israel; and the beautiful Queen of Sheba, who visited Jerusalem during the time of King Solomon.

The entire Egyptian culture was a mixture of black and white. Black cultures for thousands of years developed sophisticated societies and abilities. They were skilled in stone masonry, mining, metallurgy, and many other areas.

More than forty people from all over the state enrolled in the class, 75 percent of whom were administrators and six who were nuns. All seemed excited by this introduction to the course. Their enthusiasm put my mind at ease, and teaching the rest of the course was a breeze. I asked class members to do research on individual historic blacks. I invited guest speakers. I divided the class into teams for group projects. We had stimulating dialogues and discussions over the six-week period. One big, well-researched, well-written, and well-documented notebook was the outcome. And they *did* begin to teach black history all over the state. To make sure it was as thorough and as useful as possible, I formed an advisory committee for each area so each school could say what books they'd like to use. They chose the books and methods they wanted, using our curriculum as a guide. Eventually this course was called the History of Black America.

There were requests from forty colleges and universities for the curriculum. As I've traveled around the country since then, a number of times I've found the curriculum still in use.

Vandalism

One of the most controversial bills I was involved with was one to hold parents responsible for vandalism committed by their children in public buildings. Some thought it was abusive to the poor, but it turned out that the children of the rich often were the vandals in question. It was not a popular bill, but I felt strongly that parents needed to take more responsibility for their children. How many more kids could be trained and educated if we could spend less money on vandalism and more on education? This bill passed the next year.

Hitting Home and Heart

The legislation that passed during my tenure that meant the most to me was the fair housing bill. To me, not being able to rent a place or own property is one of the cruelest problems anyone can suffer. It eats away at your self-confidence and sense of security. It takes away your future and your hope.

The Civil Rights Act of 1968 passed by Congress had extended previous civil rights guarantees to housing and real estate. But it merely set minimum standards. It was up to local leaders to secure these rights in detail at the state level. Passing a similar bill in Iowa would mean a great deal to the process because such a law is most effective when it is supported at the local level and when it addresses state conditions. Several efforts had been made before and failed.

When Governor Hughes heard I was going to put it up for consideration, he sent me a note saying, "We've been trying to make it happen for a long time. Good luck to you." I sought out other legislators who were interested in such a bill and set to work describing what we wanted to happen. Then, our researchers sent around the country for the best bills written on fair housing. We based our bill on these and then designed our strategy. In committee, I proposed a bill that would make it illegal to deny renting or selling property to a person because of his or her race. Anyone who did would be subject to being sued and would likely lose. The real-estate board was against the bill, as were most landowners, because they feared that blacks would file numerous "nuisance" suits. They feared that there'd be many charges filed that would cost realtors and the government a lot of money to investigate, prosecute, and defend. So they amended the bill to require a deposit of $500 which would be forfeited if the complainant did not carry through on the charges.

I objected to the amount of the deposit on the grounds that such a high sum would put it out of range for the average person. I asked the committee to cut it to $250. Here again, I got some good advice on how to get things done. I was told, "Get the bill on the books and you can amend it later." June Franklin, a Democrat and the only other black legislator in office at that time, strongly disagreed with compromising. It wasn't easy going up against her; she was an effective legislator and highly respected because she was always well prepared and was a persuasive speaker. I understood why she felt that a $250 deposit would keep poor people from getting their rights. But I knew it was the only way to get the bill passed, and I was confident that the $250 would be reduced later.

This experience taught me a valuable lesson: I'll take half a loaf, a slice, or a crumb, and it will later develop into something better than you expected. My fellow legislators promised me that next year they'd get that requirement struck. I was gone by then, but they kept their word. I also learned how important the committee process is. That's where you discover the weaknesses and strengths of your proposal. If you can't work out the details there, you have a poor chance of getting it through the House and Senate.

Help in the Senate

I thought I'd have more trouble getting the fair housing bill through the House than the Senate, so I enlisted the help of two friends in the Senate, Tom Riley, a Republican, and John Ely, a Democrat. Both of them were from Cedar Rapids, and I had known them for some time. Ely, of Quaker Oats, was totally unpretentious, a real gentleman. One day I needed a ride to Des Moines, and he offered to pick me up. It was freezing cold, and he arrived in an old car with the right front window broken and covered by a blanket. It was a cold 130-mile drive to Des Moines. Riley was a respected and conservative attorney. Together they made a balanced team to present this very controversial bill.

They presented it in the Senate, and it passed with only eight dissenting votes. When I presented it in the House, the place was packed. The nuns from Mt. Mercy were there, as were Ev and Davey, the Chamber of Commerce, and everyone for or against it. It was standing room only.

The Speaker of the House said, "What's the next bill?" The Reader of the House then read the title and number of the bill and its intent. As the lead sponsor of the bill, I introduced it by explaining what we were trying to accomplish with it. Then the opponents picked it apart while the supporters jumped to its defense. This went on for about three hours. The Speaker then called for a vote. I could have asked for more time, but I felt the debate was exhausted. At issue was the amount required to file a complaint against a landlord. We proposed $250, but the opponents claimed that it was too little to avoid "frivolous and capricious complaints." So we agreed to a compromise, and I made the closing remarks. When I finished, there was a standing ovation. Before we went into session, the House clerk said, "You'll never get this passed. If you do, I'll buy you a steak." When the vote was taken, he slammed down his pen, and I knew it had passed.

When members vote, they do so by pushing a button that turns on a light, red for no and green for yes. There were no red lights that day. It passed unanimously. What a glorious day. I'd never seen such emotion as swept through the chambers; everyone was crying and hugging.

After Passage

In the aftermath of the bill's passage, it seemed that all kinds of people and organizations were interested in it. The *Cedar Rapids Gazette* commented, "Iowa legislators have displayed bipartisan statesmanship in passing a fair housing bill which reflects, we believe, the wishes of most citizens of this state. The measure has neither the hysterical overtones of delayed righteousness in the human equality movement, nor the cynical appendages that could shackle its effectiveness." News of the bill even made *JET* magazine.

Regarding my speech, I received a letter from Clarence F. Schmarje, president of Schmarje Tool Company and as conservative as they come. He said, "Your entire speech is the best example of real rhetoric that I have heard in a long time. I think it rates with those of Senator Dirksen and President Kennedy." Although I appreciated the compliment, I felt I had a long way to go to be compared to those great statesmen. Schmarje was in the House that day and told me privately, "I knew that blacks played an important role in history, but I've never heard it spelled out so well as you have done."

When the bill finally passed, I thought about all the people before me who had a part in this victory. I thought what a lonely struggle it must have been for some of the earliest. For instance,

Iowa Governor Harold Hughes is shown here signing the Fair Housing Bill in 1967. After it had been presented and discussed on the floor of the legislature, I spoke on its behalf and was given a standing ovation. A more important gift to me was that it passed unanimously.

Adam Clayton Powell, the black congressman from New York, served twenty-five years in the United States Congress and frequently aggravated his colleagues by introducing the "Powell amendment." This was a rider designed to force government contractors to provide equal employment opportunities to all races. Powell was berated by many. He was a flamboyant preacher for the Abyssinian Baptist Church in Harlem, and his personal life made the headlines frequently. But he was still an effective congressman—and a fiery fly in the buttermilk.

After Hours

While I was getting the bill passed, the phones rang constantly. I was never harassed by lobbyists, but sometimes I'd get nuisance calls all night long, just trying to wear me down I guess. I was staying at the YMCA since we had not moved from Cedar Rapids.

Luckily for me, many of the pages in the legislature lived there, too. When they heard what was happening, they said, "We'll swap rooms with you. The phone doesn't bother us."

I liked staying at the Y. It was only $35 a week, and they had a swimming pool, Ping-Pong, workout equipment, a viewing room for television, and good, cheap food ($2 a meal). I liked being with the pages, too. They'd vie to drive my car to the car wash. And we had some fiercely competitive Ping-Pong games. One of my most challenging opponents became a scientist. He wrote to me a few years ago and said, "Not only did you teach us about human rights, but you beat the heck out of me in table tennis." I needed these kids for their fresh and honest viewpoints, and they kept me from getting too lonely for my family. Some weekends I didn't get home, I was speaking all over the state and country. I was in demand, but not just because I was black at a time when civil rights was a national concern. After all, there were other blacks in the legislature. And I don't think it was because I was the "novel" black—the only Republican. I believe it was because I was writing bills that got to the heart of what really bothered people.

Early Departure

During the fifth month that I was in the legislature, four men from the governor's office were dispatched to the floor of the House with a message from the governor "to have Cecil Reed report to me immediately." They escorted a surprised and nervous Cecil Reed to his office. When I walked in, they showed me where to be seated.

I felt like I'd been sent to the principal's office. I was pretty sure I hadn't done anything wrong, but I was nevertheless slightly uneasy. Governor Hughes came in a few minutes later and told me that he wanted me to leave the legislature the last day of June so I could become head of the Iowa Employment Security Commission (now known as Job Service). That would give me a month to finish everything I had under way. I thanked him and said I'd like the opportunity. I'd never heard of anyone telling the governor "no" when he asked them to do something. Besides, it was

Robert Ray succeeded Harold Hughes as governor and appointed me to the Governor's Educational Advisory Committee. As a result, I later worked with the Board of Educational Broadcasting doing a TV and radio series on black history. This was the first time I realized that television broadcasters used prompters. I did it the old-fashioned way . . . with my memory. Notice how I'm sporting a "bush" here, the hairstyle that was popular with young blacks at the time. I adopted this hairdo after an incident with my boys. They came home from college one Christmas with "bushes," and I was raising the devil with them. Finally, Dick said, "I thought you'd be more interested in what's inside our heads than on the outside." When I saw their grade point averages, I decided he was right . . . and took up the style myself.

the highest appointment for state office ever held by a black in Iowa history—and the highest pay for state office by a black, according to the *Des Moines Register*.

Governor Robert D. Ray, who replaced Governor Hughes that fall, sent me a letter announcing that he had appointed me "with pleasure" to the Governor's Educational Advisory Committee because of my record. This, too, was a great honor and opportunity, but since it was a nonpaying appointment, it involved a considerable sacrifice in terms of money and time. But that is what it means to be a public servant. Besides, it was another chance to be involved in exciting, interesting, and rewarding work.

Bittersweet Parting

During my brief stay in the House, I learned so much, took in so much, it was almost frightening. I didn't try to figure out where it was going or how to organize it. Changes, opportunities, and problems were too many to be analyzed. I just trusted that there was some purpose, some higher reason for my being there. If I'd tried to plan or control the details, I might have limited the outcome. While I was thrilled that the governor had such faith in me, I was sad to leave behind the many friends and colleagues I'd worked with. And the honors and recognition they bestowed upon me made it even harder.

One honor came from Maurice Berringer, who was Speaker of the House. He was going to be out of the state and said, "I'd like you to be Speaker for the day." By then I knew parliamentary procedures, but even if I hadn't, I knew I could cover the microphone and ask the clerk for help. The clerk was a brilliant fellow who knew what was proper and had a great memory for everything that happened in the House. But one of the most touching moments was when I read a newspaper article saying that "the House secretaries are lamenting over his departure from the legislature because they are going to miss Mr. Reed's emotional speeches." Even though the six months I spent in the legislature went by quickly, they were long for me and long in terms of the body's history. It was the longest session in the history of the legislature.

When the governor appointed me to the commission, I had

I became the first black in history to preside over the Iowa House of Representatives. The regular Speaker of the House, Maurice Berringer, a Republican from Oelwein, turned the gavel over to me for thirty minutes shortly before I left the legislature.

promised to start by July 1. But the session was still running on my last day. So they stopped the session and had a going-away party for me. They brought in food from Kentucky Fried Chicken and made a round of farewell speeches saying that I'd done a good job.

Working with all those lobbyists, voters, organizations, and politicians during those long six months was preparation for the job before me. Little did I realize that they would be the very people I would need to help our commission put people to work. All the projects I'd worked on gave me expertise and contacts to deal with training, educating, and employing people. I have to believe there was a higher plan guiding me through the long six months to what would come next.

12   Working with Work

In July 1967, I began serving the six-year term to which Governor Hughes had appointed me as commissioner for the Iowa Employment Security Commission. I know this sounds like some sort of a protection unit, but actually it's what is now known as Job Service (although in other states it is called by other names).

It was a big shift for me to make. All my life I'd been an entrepreneur. I'd worked at every kind of job imaginable, for others and for myself, always providing some specific service or a product to customers. Now, I was working with employment. For the next twenty years, I held various positions with both the state and federal departments of labor. My work was selling ideas and methods for helping people get jobs. And it was a labor of love.

Personal Shifts

The new job required some major changes in my personal life, too. Ev and I moved to Des Moines. Davey was fifteen and the only child to move with us. Mike, nineteen, was majoring in English and physical education at the University of Northern Iowa. Carol, twenty-eight, was back in college at the University of Iowa and was raising three children by herself. Dick was twenty-four and married. He'd always been our mainstay in the businesses, so we turned them over to him. It helped that when we moved back to town four years previously, we had sold the country property to the city of Cedar Rapids. They enlarged the park and ultimately made a nature trail out of it. We felt like it was put to good use, and it made the move to a different city a little easier.

It wasn't easy for blacks to move into the nice residential areas of Des Moines in those days. But from my time in the legislature, I knew Senator Howard Reppert, who had a house at 912 Thirty-eighth Street. He rented it to us, and we liked it so well we later bought it from him. He was a great landlord and friend: he took all the rent we had paid and used it as a down payment. A coincidence about that house struck me as funny: the house number, 912, was the same as the first home my folks ever owned, 912 S. Fifth Street, in Cedar Rapids.

Another really strange thing happened with Senator Reppert. He was a spiffy dresser with a lively personality. He drove a lavender convertible with a white top. Years later, Evelyn and I were in Florida staying at the Lido Beach Holiday Inn. I looked out the window and saw a lavender convertible with a white top. We went down to check it out, and sure enough, the name on the mailbox where the car was parked was Reppert. I looked up his name and address in the phone book and gave him a call. We couldn't get over how odd it was to meet again thousands of miles away. He and his wife entertained us royally the rest of our stay.

Commencing as Commissioner

My first days as commissioner were pretty hectic, almost frightening. I had so much to learn, and I felt a special responsibility to do well. I was the first black in the United States to become an employment security commissioner. I had the overall responsibility for the administration of three major Iowa government programs: the state unemployment insurance program, the employment service program, and the Iowa Public Employees Retirement System (IPERS). Because federal funds are involved in operating these programs, the commission I headed had to meet federal standards as well as comply with state practices. The commission had the final responsibility for making sure thirty-four local employment service offices and eleven area claims centers operated efficiently and economically. At that time, approximately 26,000 Iowa employers participated in the unemployment insurance program which protected about 720,000 Iowa workers. In addition, the commission acted as an agent for the federal government in administering an unemployment insurance program to federal civilian employees and for military veterans.

The dollar figures were even more staggering. In 1968 our unemployment insurance trust fund totaled $126,380,462, and that fiscal year $13,036,087 was paid out in benefits to unemployed Iowans. The retirement system covered 120,000 former and current public employees, and the trust fund amounted to approximately $280,000,000 by the end of the 1968 fiscal year.

In a nutshell, I oversaw 550 employees at local and state levels who provided employment services to the entire state of Iowa! The activities of the commission for which I was responsible directly and indirectly affected the lives of almost every Iowan. Is it any wonder I felt somewhat intimidated? But despite my lack of knowledge about the day-to-day operation of government, at least I was able to bring a fresh point of view to the job. I had done every kind of work imaginable, and I had started numerous suc-

Here are two fly in the buttermilk photos to illustrate that even after we left Cedar Rapids, I was often the only black present in a group. Above, I am with a group of Employment Service commissioners from all over the country in 1967. Below, I'm pictured with a group from the Purdue Old Masters Program. Those in the back row were teachers, and the others were our student hosts. During a five-day period, we spoke to almost all Purdue graduate and undergraduate classes. In the evenings we dined with them in their residence halls and conducted informal question and answer sessions.

cessful businesses. I understood the problems of the employee and the employer; I understood the average citizen's bewilderment with government procedures. I was determined to make the commission's operation more responsive to the needs of the people by helping the civil servants I oversaw understand their value to the system. Over the next twenty years, I held many different positions in the state and federal departments of labor. As an administrator, I proposed and effected many changes, but I could not have done any of it without the fine secretaries I had throughout my career: Alma Gerdus, Mary Evans, Betty Parrot, and Kay Robinson. Their expertise and efficiency enabled me to do what I do best: explain the "people side" of government. I told the public what civil servants do and how well they do it; I described to government employees how they could make a real difference in the lives of every citizen they encountered by caring about each one as an individual. This is how I began my career as a public servant, and it is still my mission today.

Job Hopping

When you look at my résumé, you might wonder whether I was a reliable person. If I ever listed all my jobs, you might say I was a job hopper. But the truth is, I moved in and out of many positions within one business and often held simultaneous jobs. I've thought a lot about this business of job hopping, and I've come to think of it as "flexible employment" instead.

All of this came to me one day when I'd first started my job with the Department of Labor. A young man came to visit me who was the son of some people I knew. He was working at a fast-food operation. He wanted me to help him get a loan. I told him I didn't do that for my own children, and I asked why he was leaving the job he had. He said it was a high turnover job with no future. I told him that it had been my experience that where the turnover was highest, the opportunities were greatest. I said, "If you stay there and learn all the jobs they have, you'll soon become the manager."

Well, he took my advice and became a very successful manager. Not long afterward, I read in the paper that he was quite a hero, too. Two fellows who didn't know he was a karate expert tried to rob the restaurant. He disarmed them and held them until the police came. The police lectured him about how dangerous it was for him to disarm them. But he was not persuaded. He said, "As long as I'm manager, there ain't nothing leaving here but chicken." You can tell that he was a dedicated, determined employee who job-hopped his way to success.

Moving On

All this is a slightly apologetic explanation of why I served only three years of my appointment as job commissioner until I shifted jobs. In 1969 I became the executive assistant for the Regional Administrator for Equal Opportunity, Department of Labor. That's a mouthful, but basically what it means is that I moved from state administration to regional administration and thereby from a state to a federal employee. I became the Equal Opportunity Employment Specialist for the Kansas City Manpower Administration.

The region I covered was huge. It now encompasses Regions 7 and 8 and included ten states: Colorado, Iowa, Kansas, Missouri, Montana, Nebraska, Nevada, North and South Dakota, and Utah. And I traveled throughout those states. I recall being in cold, snowy Montana one day and burning up in Las Vegas a few days later. And I performed many roles. I remember reviewing the records of Montana employment agencies one week and the next week setting up programs in Las Vegas that taught people how to deal cards and handle drunk patrons. I loved the diversity of the people and problems I dealt with.

This was a time in our country's history when the administrative branch of the government was trying to put into practice the laws previously enacted by the legislative branch regarding civil rights. I was assistant to William S. Harris, the regional Manpower administrator, and my charge was to help him carry out the agency's responsibilities to implement "the letter and spirit of Title VI of the Civil Rights Act of 1964." Simply stated, Title VI was designed to prevent discrimination against minorities in employment. Title VII established the Equal Employment Opportunity Commission as a means of effecting the intentions of Title

VI. As an EEO Specialist, I handled discrimination complaints against Job Service and its programs in Regions 7 and 8. According to my job description, my duties were to investigate complaints of discrimination in employment, train Employment Service agency employees in matters related to EEO issues, conduct preaward reviews of potential federal contractors to determine whether they were likely to comply with EEO standards regarding employment of minorities, analyze reports of Employment Service agencies and the employers they worked with to identify and correct deficiencies, and represent the Regional Manpower Administration at meetings and conferences involving the EEO or assistance to minority groups.

Name of the Game

Communication was the real name of the game. It was a touchy business trying to get employers and unions to eliminate discriminatory practices. They were just trying to do business as usual and "all of a sudden the government started meddling." I honestly believe that most cases of discrimination stemmed not from bigotry but simply because changing the way they operated required time, money, and energy they didn't want to expend.

Because of my experiences in business as an employee and as an employer, I understood their feelings. I believe this helped me to help them ease into compliance. I could sympathetically explain to them what had to be done and how they could do it. The same experiences helped me talk to unions and convince them to accept more minorities as apprentices. Of course, it didn't hurt that I was a member of the Carpenter's Union.

I think it also helped that I had spoken to more than 350 groups across the nation on equal opportunity and the dignity of work. I designed a special plan for interviewing the hard-core unemployed that was used successfully in the Des Moines Employment Program Center. I was interviewed numerous times on radio and television and wrote many articles for newspapers and magazines on the problems of the disadvantaged and on minority groups. And, of course, the class on black history I initiated while I was a legislator added to my reputation. People were willing to listen to someone who was involved in the nitty-gritty details of making change happen.

At the time I created the class, I referred to it as "Negro" history and was criticized for doing so, especially by other blacks. But when the class was designed, "Negro" was the accepted term. I'd tell these critics: "You're darn right I say 'Negro.' It took twenty-five years to get them to capitalize it. Besides, you can call me black, colored, or Negro—just so you call me when you've got a job offer."

I felt the same about the shift to the term Afro-American. I can't see getting all bent out of shape about which term they use. I guess living in a time when "colored" and "nigger" were common makes you a little less concerned with what is currently politically correct.

Moving to Job Corps

In 1971 I became the assistant administrator for Job Corps and remained in that position until 1974. I was particularly excited about this opportunity to help young people become employable. I had the authority and responsibility to "make significant contributions to the development of policy at the national level and to develop significant innovations and adaptations for the success of the program at the regional level." I also was to work with prospective government contractors in the region, advising them on how to prepare their proposals.

Here again, communication was important. My main job was to coordinate the activities of Job Corps with other Manpower Administration programs, with local communities, with recruitment and placement agencies, and with education and vocational training programs for youth. And as before, I was blessed with a talented, hardworking staff and the most accomplished deputy I've ever known, John Douglas. They made it possible for me to concentrate on visiting and monitoring on a continual basis the total operation of Job Centers in the region, as well as Job Corps programs such as Conservation Centers, Urban Centers, Residential Manpower Centers, and Residential Support Centers.

When I found that offices and programs were not operating as they should, it was my job to recommend corrective action. One Job Service Center in the region was an old, run-down facility, with few programs and low morale; no one wanted to go there. I said to an assistant, Jack Goss, "Turn this into a good center that people will want to come to." The first thing he did was to get Job Corps students to construct a new great-looking building for the center. When it opened, he arranged for me to speak to the local union and ask them to visit the center. We were a little surprised that they accepted so readily. Everyone was excited. They got an entertainment program together, and the culinary students made a catfish dinner complete with salad and hush puppies.

The union people turned out in droves and had a great time. The carpenters crawled under the building to see how the kids had repaired the floors. They talked to the youngsters about work and took a great interest in the center, so much so that they took many of the kids on as apprentices.

One union man taught our Job Corps youngsters how to use heavy equipment in the same way many university coaches train their football teams—he "coached" them from a tower, radioing instructions to them in the field. Because of his training, that center got such a good reputation for heavy equipment operators that companies in other states hired them. When he asked one of his trainees why he decided to go to New Mexico for a job offer, the young man said, "$10.50 an hour." So you can see they also learned something about finances.

Employment and Training

The diversity of my work at Job Service prepared me for my next job as assistant regional administrator, United States Department of Labor, Area Operations for Employment and Training Programs, which I assumed in December of 1974. I was responsible for Employment and Training Administration activities under the Comprehensive Employment and Training Act of 1973 (CETA). To a certain extent this move was merely a name change. A new administration brought a somewhat different focus, but my basic duties were still to make people employable. By this time, I'd seen how agencies operate, and I was convinced that the most helpful role I could perform was to be a cheerleader who encouraged people to operate as a team. I wanted to be sure that everyone understood how important they were to the effective operation of the agency.

During this time, I was the liaison between federal policymakers and those in the region who applied the policies. My staff monitored the operation of such agencies as Youth Employment Service, Job Corps, and Veterans Employment and Training. I served in this capacity until 1979, when I became the Assistant Regional Administrator for Job Service. Basically, I performed the same duties as those in my first Job Service position, except that now I was covering the region instead of just the state of Iowa and I was a federal employee instead of state. I served in that capacity until I retired in 1983.

In an effort to make it as brief and clear as possible, I have omitted many details from this description of my twenty-year career in government. I did not list the "acting" capacities I served in. For a while I was Deputy Administrator for Region 7. Once I was the grants officer who signed off on contracts for the states and cities that met our requirements. I was once the certifying officer for immigration, which made me responsible for seeing to it that immigrants would not take jobs away from United States citizens.

Holding these different positions was good experience for me—but it sounds confusing to the uninitiated. Anyone who feels that government service is a rigid, boring, dead-end career track simply doesn't understand how it operates. Because of continual political and economic changes, government is always in a state of flux. Agency names, objectives, funding, and personnel change frequently. Therefore, job titles and program purposes are in a constant state of flux. While this is unsettling at times, it also means there is constant opportunity to learn, grow, advance, and perform a useful service.

This is partly due to changes in administrations. When there is a new president, governor, legislator, or mayor, they have different agendas from their predecessors and immediately set to work changing the structure of the bureaus and agencies that put their ideas into effect. Another reason for the constantly changing titles and duties of public servants is that the government in our country tries to and does respond to the changing needs and desires of the public. When there is a period of high employment and wages, the Department of Labor's role might be to refine labor relations strategies and to encourage development of vocational education. But when unemployment rates are high and inflation is rampant, the department's role typically shifts to devising programs to help the unemployed and homeless.

Extracurricular Activities

As a businessman and a legislator, I worked on many public committees and with many organizations. All this provided me with a network of friends and associates with all kinds of interests, talents, and resources. When I entered government service, it seemed even more important to continue these activities because they kept me in touch with the public. Eventually, this network became a national one, because of the people I talked to all over this country and because of the groups I worked with outside my official job.

For example, in 1968 I became chairman of the Iowa division of the United Nations Human Rights Committee and served on the board of directors of the national association. In this volunteer job I met many national and international leaders, including Arthur Goldberg, Everett Dirksen, Hubert Humphrey, Ray Marshall, and many leaders in industry and unions. This added to my political stature and extended my network. I was getting to know people throughout the region and the country. I could see how systems work—and how I could accomplish good things by acting on behalf of all people.

In 1968 I started the Northern Brotherhood Leadership Conference (NBLC). I felt that the word "Christian" in Ralph Abernathy's Southern Christian Leadership Conference excluded Jewish people. I wanted to offer an alternative—a new organization with wide-ranging plans for breaking down racial barriers.

More than two hundred people attended that first meeting, most of them white. I described the purpose of the organization and laid out an eight-point plan for overcoming racial barriers.

During my years in government service, I met and worked with many well-known public figures. Here are some of my favorites: Whitney Young, the Urban League; Roy Wilkins, the NAACP; Janet Rockefeller, wife of the Arkansas governor, Winthrop Rockefeller; and Dr. Bonita Washington, wife of Washington, D.C., Mayor Walter Washington. Dr. Washington was a dynamic speaker who served as superintendent of schools in Washington, D.C., and was assistant administrator for Job Corps.

The result was a vital organization that succeeded in opening many doors in Iowa and other parts of the country. Even though it doesn't exist today, I feel sure and proud that it helped midwesterners face the problems of integration during those troubled times.

The Power of Speech

There were many other organizations that I spoke to and activities that I participated in throughout my career in government. But public speaking afforded me the greatest opportunity to reach the most people. Along the way, I got help from some pretty high-powered people. For instance, the first time I spoke outdoors was at a chautauqua meeting in Chadron, Nebraska, in June 1975. Chautauqua is the name of an adult education program that originated in the United States in the 1870s. These programs would travel to different sites around the country and eventually became the first successful correspondence education program in the United States. They featured popular lectures, concerts, and dramatic productions and traditionally were held in tents.

The Nebraska chautauqua had a tent to cover the speakers while the audience sat in bleachers or on the ground. Unfortunately, the weather was cold and wet. My vocal cords became infected, and I lost my voice. Douglas Edwards, the fine and famous broadcaster, reached in his pocket, gave me a lemon, and said, "Bite into this." It was miraculous. I was able to present my entire speech and take questions from the audience. This is another tradition of the chautauqua: when the speaker is finished, the audience gets to ask you questions about what you've said. Whenever possible, the same group of speakers would appear together at different chautauqua locations. The group I spoke with included Attorney General Ramsey Clark (under Lyndon Johnson), Douglas Edwards, Will Rogers, Jr., and Nebraska Governor J. James Exon.

Some of my other speaking engagements were less exalted. During one of my campaign speeches, I noticed a ripple of laughter going around the room. I looked over the rostrum and saw a very pregnant white woman sitting in the front row under a sign that said, "Cecil's the One." It's a good thing I can't blush or I would have been beet red.

My walls are filled with plaques, trophies, and certificates, many of which were presented to me at these speaking engagements. They are too numerous to mention. But wherever and to whomever I spoke, each speech and each award was and is important to me. Although I cannot remember the names of every person I've hugged or talked to over the years, each one made a difference in my life.

Rules of Thumb

Here are some things I learned about working as an administrator in government that I think work just as well in the private sector and one's personal life as they did for me in government.

Turn them loose. Free the people who work for you to do what they know best. They have so much talent and experience, but many times no one has ever given them the power and confidence to do it. For instance, administrators often didn't want to talk to my assistant whose job title was secretary. So I just changed her title to "executive assistant." After that, she handled most of my phone calls, probably more efficiently than I.

Write letters of appreciation. I was always free with compliments, and I put them on paper. We all like compliments, but spoken ones fade from the memory. When it's on paper, you can go back years later and still get the same good feeling you had when it was first given. When you send these letters, make sure they reach the person's personnel files where they'll count at promotion time.

Ask for and use the help of your subordinates. You can't know it all, you need others. Don't be afraid to admit you don't know everything. Others will respect your honesty and be happy to demonstrate their expertise.

Say it with love. This is something my mom, Julia Reed, always practiced. When people make mistakes, tell them about it with love. When you're making a tough decision that will hurt someone, make it with love, and they won't be hurt so much by it.

Commingle money with other agencies and offices. The money goes farther and you get more done. In government, funding often shifts from one department or agency to another. When you've got it, share it with like-minded operations. Then when they've got it, maybe they'll help you out. It also cuts down on duplication of efforts and watering down of available funds.

Commingling might not sound practical in the competitive business world, but it can work. I know in the field of consulting, many of my colleagues help each other get new clients. We all have specialties and limitations. When I come across a client who needs a consultant outside my field, I recommend someone who's qualified. I've satisfied my customer's need and helped another consultant. And usually, somewhere down the road, that consultant will help me. This idea is the underlying concept of what is now called networking.

Don't take changes personally. When the power (usually gauged by money) shifts from your agency to another, don't take it personally. Show them how you can work with them to make *them* look good. Inevitably, new legislatures will fiddle with an agency's organization and funding. Don't feel defeated. Find ways to help the new power, and you'll find the job will get done—even though you're not the top power this time.

In the private sector, when economic and social factors change drastically and your product or service becomes obsolete, look around and see how you can profit from the power shift. For example, when Prohibition was enacted, the Coors Beer Company in Golden, Colorado, shifted to producing malt for candy and malted milk drinks. As a result, they never had to lay off anyone.

Don't accept limitations. Whether you're working for yourself, in private industry, or for the government, don't give up on your ideas and enthusiasms. When you have a good way of doing things, push to get it your way. There is a way to fulfill your dreams whether you're in or out of government, in the private or public sector.

Love your work. W.G., my dad, always said, "You're respected for the work you do." Those who are happiest are happy in their work. Those who are happiest in their work feel they have a say in what they do. So if you see a problem, do something about it.

Keep this in mind when you're managing others; give them as much power over their own time and work as possible. They'll get more done and feel better about doing it.

Love what you do and the money will come. I agree with the book, *Do What You Love and the Money Will Come,* but sometimes you have to kiss a lot of frogs in between. Most jobs have unpleasant sides to them, but if you perform your job in the best way possible, the job grows, changes, and improves. I'm always challenged by work, no matter how menial. I like to find a better way of doing it. I like to add my personal touch.

I guess I was influenced in this by my fifth-grade English teacher, Miss Lucille Owens. She saw me struggling to feel good about myself in an all-white class. She discovered that I could write poetry and designated me the poet laureate of the class. A few times I thought this wasn't a favor to a kid named Cecil. I had a few scraps over that one. But she taught me to have pride in my abilities and to always do the best job possible. Her philosophy was summed up in the final two lines of a poem by Douglas Malloch that she used to recite to us: "It isn't by size that you win or fail / Be the best of whatever you are."

13 The Other Side of Bureaucracy

Several years ago in the Denver airport, I overheard a fellow say to another, "Hi, I'm from the federal government. I'm here to help you." And they both laughed it up. Biggest joke you ever heard . . . making fun of the government and bureaucrats. Since I had to wait a little while for my ride downtown, I said, "Let me talk to you about that joke. Let me tell you about bureaucracy and your government. I was there for twenty years. I've been in the private and the public sector; I've met people from all over. I didn't see these lazy people you talk about. I didn't see the paper shufflers you laugh at. I saw people doing what the president and Congress told them to do. They enforce the laws, rules, and regulations of this great nation. And they do it so well that other nations try to copy it."

Now I was really on a roll, so I continued, "When there's a forest fire or an earthquake or a hurricane, nobody laughs when the Department of Agriculture, the Coast Guard, FEMA disaster relief, Civil Defense, or the Small Business Administration sends in 'government people' to help. No, you call your congressmen, you call the president, and you say, 'Hurry up and get the bureaucrats out here.' And when there's a serious health problem such as AIDS, you turn to the United States Department of Health—a bureaucracy. Speaking of health, government research brought us plastic corneas that give back your 20–20 vision and laser technology that performs bloodless surgery. It was a bureaucrat who invented the CAT scan, which doctors use to diagnose cancer, brain disorders, and other diseases.

"People say that our government is slow and bogged down in red tape. But remember when President Kennedy told the bureaucrats, 'I want this country to go to the moon in ten years'? The bureaucrats did it in eight years. The first U.S. female in space was Sally Ride—a teacher and bureaucrat. The first person to walk on the moon, Neil A. Armstrong—a bureaucrat. And Lt. Thornton, the first black in space. And bureaucratic research opened the way for new products and businesses: dehydrated and frozen foods and the plastic wrap and Teflon to store and cook them in; solid state technology that led to transistor radios and miniature TVs; improved electronics used in solar-driven calculators and watches; sweatsuits and sport shoes that came from NASA's moonwalking inventions. Bureaucrats found titanium and other new, stronger, lighter metals which allow fishermen to increase their catches by 30 percent. In their search to unlock the mysteries of the universe, the scientists in the NASA bureaucracy discovered the first black hole. And how about the heat for nuclear fission—that's the work of those bureaucrats at the Department of Energy. And bureaucrats made the first modern computer, instrument landing systems used by all commercial and military aircraft, as well as the basic design of most aircraft."

By this time, those two guys had stopped laughing, and they were begging me to stop. In fact, they said, "If you'll just shut up, we promise never to joke about bureaucrats again." I laughed, and we parted friends. I really didn't blame them. Until you've been in government work, it's hard to understand how dedicated the people are and what good work they do.

A Bias for Bureaucracy

I had no particular bias for or against government workers until I became one of them. Once I entered the public sector, I developed a strong bias *for* bureaucrats. I spent twice as many years working for myself as for the government, but I saw more entrepreneurs in bureaucracy. I saw people who performed heroically, working with limited time, funds, and staffing. I saw enthusiastic and inventive government employees who could not have performed their work except through willpower and creativity.

I'm thinking about the women who work for city, county, state, and federal agencies all over this country. They do their jobs all day, then most of the work at home. Mildred C. Parsons in the FBI's Washington, D.C., field office must hold the world's record for commitment. She served forty-five years without missing a single working day, without taking one day of sick leave. American women at all levels have brought excellence and dedication to government work. Then, too, I think about some people I worked with in CETA, such as Tom Youngworth. He and other bureaucrats would travel all over the region or attend meetings all day long . . . then they'd be writing their reports late at night. There's no overtime pay in government work.

I think, too, of the military people I've known. I love to be around them. They carry themselves in a way that makes me have confidence in them. They're neat, polite, clean and have a "can do" attitude. Those who say the military mind is rigid ought to meet John Elkins or Lee McCormick or Bob Hale, all former military people I've worked with at the Department of Labor. They know how to work under pressure. They're inventive, efficient, and loyal. They put their egos aside and work for the good of the team.

Programs

People are also cynical about government programs. They call them boondoggles. But we'd miss a lot without them. More than 95 percent of our schoolchildren are protected against major vaccine-preventable diseases by government-sponsored inoculation and vaccination programs. Reported cases of diphtheria, measles, mumps, polio, and rubella have reached all-time lows. In a typical year, some 225,000 young runaways are served by the National Runaway Hotline, and the Federal School Lunch Program helps feed 12.3 million schoolchildren. For some, it's the only balanced meal they get that day.

And how about the training and education our bureaucracy provides? Fifty-two percent of public employees at the state and local level work at educating people. Some 425,000 children are enrolled in the federally staffed Head Start programs. Fifty percent of all the doctors in the United States are trained in the Veterans Administration by bureaucrats.

But I'm not just talking about million-dollar programs or the bureaucrats who have made headlines. I'm thinking about the day-by-day operation of the government and the thousands of nameless people who keep it going. And they do it efficiently and often on their own time. The Public Employees Roundtable, a nonprofit educational organization representing a coalition of twenty-one professional employee groups, reports that each year federal government employees contribute approximately $600 million of uncompensated overtime to taxpayers. While the workload has increased many times over, the number of federal government employees has been decreasing since 1969.

Bureaucrats help us behave and keep the whole system running. Sure there are glitches in the system. There are laggards and clock-watchers, but on the whole, we have the best government in the world.

A Flexible Bureaucracy

We have good people who make the system function. I found that our form of civil service really does work for the good of the public. The rank-and-file employees usually stay with their departments during changes in leadership. They provide the continuity that keeps our government operating day in and day out. Now, it's different with administrators. They move around a lot . . . and they provide the changes and movement that keep government from becoming static and unresponsive. Both elements are vital to keeping our government operating in a predictable yet flexible way.

When you look at the failure of the Soviet Union, you can see the advantages of our system. In the Soviet Union, administrations and administrators never changed. So there was never a challenge to the status quo. Heads never rolled. Policies never changed. The only thing that changed was red tape . . . and it grew. The Berlin Wall came down because people got tired of not having the kinds of goods and services we have. The same thing happened in the Soviet Union and is starting to happen all over the world. Americans have one of the lowest tax rates of any country and one of the most complex yet efficient government structures. Along with Canada, the Netherlands, and Japan, we have the fewest public-sector employees in relation to the size of the economy. Only Japan spends less of its gross domestic product on government than we do. Think how that figure would change if they couldn't count on us for their national defense.

The mention of Japan reminds me of one last thing I have to say about our bureaucracy and bureaucrats. I get upset when people compare us unfavorably to the Japanese. They prosper in part because their population is so homogeneous. They fall in step once the direction has been laid out for them by their government. It's much more difficult in this country because our population is so diverse. It's a great challenge to administer programs and services to people from many different backgrounds. But it's worth the trouble. Ask any geneticist what happens when you mix two different strains of grain: you get a hybrid—a stronger, better product. It's the same with ideas and ways of doing things. Variety produces stronger, better methods. We have lots of variety and strength in our people and our government.

I've worked with groups and individuals in every part of the country and every sector of the government—from the highest administrative level to the lowest entry-level positions, from the scientists in the Department of Agriculture and NASA to the Office of Personnel Management and the Internal Revenue Service. Without exception, they have been sincere, caring, talented people.

So the next time you hear someone say, "It's close enough for government work," speak up for bureaucrats. Remind the person of some pretty important things bureaucrats have done. The next time you hear people making fun of public servants, remember that they're talking about a real person who, 99 percent of the time, is trying to do a good job. Do your part in countering the unfair things said about the folks who run our country. We'd be lost without them.

14   What Do You Tell the Children?

For the most part, you'll not find sad, hopeless stories in this book because I am a positive, hopeful man. But there is one part of my life that is so painful to recall, I want to isolate it in one chapter. It is the story of our son David. His suicide is the one roadblock I can't turn into a stepping-stone, the one scar I can't turn into a star.

David was born in 1952, our third son and fourth child. He

was a beautiful baby, big and handsome from the start. The other children loved to play with him, and he was a favorite of everyone in the neighborhood. I used to laugh at times when I'd drop him off to play with two little neighborhood girls. He'd warn me pretty seriously that the only way he'd stay was if they promised "no kissing." He grew to be the largest of our children and very good-looking. He was as nice as he was good-looking. Maybe too nice and too handsome.

Davey was full of love and happiness—until he started school. I can see now that he'd been more protected than our other children by the loving cocoon of our family and neighborhood. The others had taken some lumps and learned some hard lessons about the real world that Davey, the baby of the family, was protected from. The first five years of his life weren't much like the real world, so when he entered first grade he was unprepared for name-calling and social pressure. His trusting and sensitive nature in the face of hostility finally killed him.

I will always wonder if I could have done more to prepare and protect him. Even today, it is constantly on my mind. When David first started school I would hear him sobbing at night. I would go to his room to see what was wrong. He would beg me not to send him to school because the kids at school didn't like him the way the neighbor kids did. He told me brokenheartedly that the kids at school called him "nigger" and told him their parents said they shouldn't play with dirty people. It affected his grades and his attitude.

His unhappiness seemed to get worse each year, and Ev and I didn't know what to do. Finally, the school principal seemed to have the solution. He knew our family well and wanted to help. Even though Dave was only a third grader, the principal put Dave on the sixth-grade football team. He performed so well, it made him kind of a star. Kids being kids, they all wanted to be his friend then.

Everything changed for the better for a while. But one day at recess a teacher shouted, "The last one in is a nigger baby." These words hurt Davey a lot. He cried when he told us about it. And once the kids heard this from the teacher, the verbal violence started again.

This is Dave at eighteen, three years before he ended his life in 1973. He was tall, with the build and grace of a natural athlete. Even though his "bush" was pretty short for the styles in those days, it attracted unfavorable attention from police and other authorities. Young black men are often in harm's way just because of their appearance.

Davey became a fine football player, trackman, and wrestler. He was a fair student, but the labels continued to plague him. Even the good ones bothered him. When he played well on the ballfield people called him Jim Brown or O.J. Simpson. When he won eighteen straight track races, he was called Bob Hayes or some other track star. When he was the leading man in a school play he was called Sidney Poitier or Harry Belafonte. Davey said rather wistfully one day that he had never been called by his own name by others outside the family.

It was even worse when people made assumptions on the basis of his looks. Because he was big and had bushy hair, people assumed he was a militant even though he was never involved in a fight or other problems. He was picked up by the Des Moines police the night of Martin Luther King's death for no reason other than that many blacks and whites were causing disturbances that night. He was just riding around with a friend who got mixed up in the confusion and was driving the wrong way on a one-way street. Of course, it was unwise to be on the streets at such a time, but it was also wrong to automatically jail a passenger under such circumstances. At the same time that Davey was becoming depressed and disillusioned, the drug culture was more and more taking over college campuses. Dave began to run with the wrong crowd. He became distant and morose.

Finally, one night when he was at an all-time low, he made up his mind to kill himself. I spent the entire night talking, arguing, and wrestling with him. He had removed the blade from a safety razor and was trying to cut the large vein in his neck. I fought with him for four hours before I could take it away from him.

I was sixty-two years old at the time and he was twenty-one. He was 6 feet 1 and 220 pounds of solid muscle. I was 200 pounds and 5 feet 11. I got many cuts on my hands and arms trying to get that blade away from him. But I felt whatever happened didn't matter if I could save my baby boy. As we wrestled, I talked to him, telling him how much we loved him, how I couldn't allow him to kill himself, that I'd been told it was an unforgiveable sin. We fought in his room, out into the hall, into the bathroom.

At times I felt like giving up, but then a new surge of energy would come. After what seemed like an eternity, I got the razor blade, threw it in the toilet, and flushed it. I had hardly caught my breath when he started for the steps to the first floor. I just knew that he was headed for the kitchen to get a butcher knife.

He was already bleeding from a small wound in his neck. My hands were also bleeding, and we fought all the way down the steps through the dining room and finally into the kitchen. All the while I was asking God to help me because I was completely exhausted. He grabbed a butcher knife and put it to his neck. At that point, with all the strength I could muster, I tripped him and jerked the arm away that held the knife.

Just then Ev and our oldest son came in, and we took him to the emergency room of the hospital. They sewed up his neck wound at about 6 A.M. It seemed like the end of a long nightmare . . . but it was only the beginning.

Months later when he wanted to get off an airplane in Des Moines, he was thought to be a militant and arrested. He wasn't feeling well and was aware that his aunt (my sister) lived there in Des Moines. The plane was parked at the airport, but there was no skywalk. After everyone was on the plane, he decided to get off. He asked the hostess to open the door. She refused. When he insisted, several men tried to hold him. This was a mistake on their part. With his great strength, they had no luck with him, and so the pilot called the police. The pilot then went out and said to let him off the plane. That's when the police sprayed mace in his face and shackled him. The local police charged him with creating a disturbance.

Someone who remembered me (I still don't know who) called my wife in Kansas City and told her what had happened. I went up to get him and was told they'd been afraid he might try to blow up the plane. To them he looked like a militant. They assured me he had behaved like a real gentleman and hadn't used any bad language. The police were very nice to me and, under the circumstances, treated me with understanding and consideration. The Federal Aviation Administration agents said no harm was done. Maybe not as far as they were concerned—but the damage was done to Dave. He'd suffered a deadly humiliation.

During this time Dave was constantly up and down in his moods. But I think we really got closer than ever before. We spent night after night together, sometimes practicing karate for two or three hours at a time. It seemed to relax him and help him sleep better.

About thirty days later, I was in Washington, D.C., with a good friend, Jack Goss, on Job Corps business. Evelyn called me and told me she had found Dave in his bed with a two-inch shotgun hole in his head, the blood running through the mattress and onto his record collection.

The wounds from sticks and stones will heal, but the wounds from words will last a lifetime and maybe take your life. The Bible says, "Life and death are in the power of the tongue." As I look back on Dave's life and death, I am full of sadness and regrets. I keep trying to think what I could have done to save Dave's life. Sometimes I blame it on the drug culture and the competition of sports. Those certainly were factors, but I know in my heart that the underlying problem was labels, and that's something you can't protect your children from.

The name-calling I suffered through as a child didn't hurt me nearly as much as seeing my own children go through it. As a parent, I felt helpless. What do you tell the children when someone hurts them with names? That's the agony Ev and I suffered as we brought up our children. And with Dave, it seems like we couldn't come up with the right answer.

I realize that others might think there were other reasons for Davey's death . . . and, truly, there were other factors. But I know in my heart that the underlying reason was the many hurts that came from the insensitivity of others. Our son Mike used to be physically badgered in school. The kids would hang him upside down over the toilet stool and dip him in it. "It never stopped," he told us, "until I became a bruising football player. I took out my aggressions on the football field—and they respected me for it. When I told Davey this, he just laughed." Davey just wasn't able to toughen up emotionally. Today, thousands of young people commit suicide because they can't bear the pain of being called a "homo" or a "dork" or a "cripple."

There will always be an emptiness in our lives. I still relive those awful nights. When the phone rings in my hotel room even today, I jump and am filled with fear. Then a calm and a relief come over me when it is a voice welcoming me to town for a speech or to invite me to eat with the people I'm speaking to. I will always relive the tragedy of Davey's life and death each time the phone rings. I hope God will forgive Davey for taking his own life. I honestly believe he could only handle twenty-one years of living in those very turbulent times.

One painful outcome that I'm almost grateful for is the sensitivity I have for others now. Davey's death has caused me to hurt for those who can't walk or run or work like I have; for those who can't feel the hurt of hard work in their arms because they have none; for those who can't see the sunrise or sunset; for those who can't hear the Kansas City Symphony or the loud rhythms of the young people; for those who don't or haven't had the joy of children, their laughter and crying; for those who have lost their mates; for those brave and wonderful women who raise children alone because their men aren't "man enough" to help.

I hurt some nights and can't sleep thinking about people who have no place to sleep, people who have nothing to eat. Davey's death made me aware of the pain that so many suffer. I'm committed to making a difference in the lives of as many troubled people as possible. One of the reasons I organized the Northern Brotherhood Leadership Conference in 1968 was because I was so troubled about what was happening to families and children in those days. Changes were occurring in the neighborhoods and schools, and oftentimes these were met with verbal and physical violence.

I wrote a poem to sum up my worries and hopes. The times are similar today. Verbal violence is still hurting people. And families are more in danger than ever. Maybe this poem will remind us that our children need more care than ever before.

What Do We Tell the Children?

My neighborhood is changing from white to black,
I think somewhere in me there is a terrible lack.

And I must be more than merely annoyed.
Is there a question that I must avoid?

I know in myself I do have religion.
Tell me, oh Lord, what do I tell the children?

What Do You Tell the Children? **165**

Our school is changing to a darker hue.
My feelings about this I try to subdue.

I'm asking, oh Lord, please give me a clue.
What do I say, and what do I do?
I have to admit, I'm depending on you.

We all profess that we have good religion,
but tell me dear Lord, what do I tell the children?

My church, school, and neighborhood
are all in transition.
There must be some kind of Christian coalition,
to change this horrible kind of condition.

The people are robbing
and killing each other.
How can we stop it from going further?

There must be some hearts
that we have not reached,
a way to stop this awful division.

Please tell me what to tell the children.
You taught us to laugh, you taught us to cry.
We know how to moan, and we know how to sigh.

This we can do for all to see
for we know how things are,
and how they should be.

Some we will know,
and we must reach a decision.
For I am concerned about
how all this affects the children.

15   New Life, Old Issues

When I established 1983 as a date for retiring, I knew
I needed to find a way to continue talking to people across the
country. I felt I'd made a difference during my years of speaking
out, and I wanted to keep on making a difference.

A friend said I needed a logo for promotional materials if I
wanted to be a consultant. I had just the right thing in mind:
a symbol that would stand for networking and caring. Cecil A.
Reed would be at the top, with the "A" in the form of a bridge to

represent my desire to bridge the people-gap. I wanted to be a black voice that would be heard by all races, creeds, and political persuasions. Another friend of mine who's blind produced the logo, and I was ready to go.

Soon, I was busier than ever. My continuous involvement with government agencies, unions, and corporations for twenty-three years gave me a network that continues to grow. I find that many of those I dealt with in the early days are now the bosses, and they want me to get the message to their employees. I've never had to market my speeches. Word-of-mouth has made me one of the busiest retirees around. I speak to approximately a hundred groups a year around the nation and worldwide, from the Internal Revenue Service and Office of Personnel Management to the Job Training Partnership Administration and Department of Agriculture, plus many unions, churches, and companies.

One of my favorite regular assignments began in 1986 for the National Veterans Training Institute in Denver. This institute trains the federal employees from all over the country who help military veterans get jobs, counseling, and training. The institute's motto is "Caring Enough to Make the Difference"; they and their class participants truly do.

Reaping the Harvest

Ev and I now live in Shawnee Mission, Kansas, in the middle of the country halfway between our son Mike in California, and our daughter, Carol, in New York. The minister, Dick, lives in Cedar Rapids, which I consider my hometown.

We have grandchildren and great-grandchildren. And I have thousands of adopted loved ones around the country. Every time I speak, I make new friends and adopt new children. Every person I've hugged after a speech means something special to me.

Our move to Shawnee Mission actually started many years before, shortly after Davey died. Living in that big house, walking by his room and thinking about those sad times finally prompted us to look around for a different way to live. We decided to become urbanites and moved to a beautiful apartment in Crown

Here I am when I retired at age seventy in 1983.

Center's Santa Fe Place where everything you need is in one area.
But we found that it just wasn't us. We're countryfolk. So I called
an old friend from the days I worked for the government, Tom
Youngworth, who'd become a realtor. I told him we wanted a
place close-in that would be like living in the country. To our
delight, he found just the right place.

Shawnee Mission is a small neighborhood, a few miles from
downtown Kansas City and twenty-five miles from the airport. All
the homes have two bedrooms, and we've got one of the few with

A recent photo of Evelyn, my partner for life.

a basement. That doesn't mean that we're better off than our neighbors . . . just that we're pack rats and have lots of stuff to put in the basement. The house is a perfect size for us, and the neighbors are friendly and helpful.

Things were really different when we bought *this* house. Tom found no resistance to our moving into this white neighborhood. They didn't peek from behind the curtains to size us up or burn any crosses on our front lawn. In fact, a white man down the street shoveled my walk the first time it snowed.

Carol, our only daughter, has three children, Ted and the twins, Tony and Terry. Although she doesn't look like a grandmother, Carol has five grandchildren. Four of them are Ted's and one is Terry's. Carol lives in New York City with Terry, where both of them are involved in theatrical careers. Carol was a Phi Beta Kappa student at the University of Iowa, majoring in fine arts. When she taught journalism at the University of Missouri, Kansas City, she also choreographed theater productions. Carol later worked for the Shakespeare Festival in Shaker Heights, Ohio.

Dick, our oldest son, is a minister for the Cedar Rapids Church of Christ. When he is traveling for the church's evangelical missions, his nephew, Todd, serves as minister. Dick and Sandy, his wife, have two children, Craig and Kelly, and three grandchildren.

Mike, our middle son, is regional vice president of Prime America Insurance Company in California. He has five children, Todd, Michelle, Matthew, Justin, and Milan. This picture shows Mike when he was a student at the University of Northern Iowa, where he majored in physical education and English. He taught at North High School in Des Moines and Northeast Junior High School in Kansas City but moved into the business area after a stint at a fee-charging employment office in Flushing Meadows, New York. This, and the campus turmoil of the seventies, got him interested in troubled people, and he worked with exoffenders programs in Iowa, Arkansas, and Los Angeles. Through these programs he met many television celebrities and athletes and still works with them in a volunteer program in Los Angeles called World Impact. Its thrust is to provide education to inner-city children.

Frances, my older living sister, now lives in Des Moines at Lutheran Park Place where she keeps busy with crafts and speaking all over the state for church groups. She teaches knitting and quilting. A prize-winning quilt she made hangs in the sanctuary of St. John's Lutheran Church. At eighty-six she is amazing: her eyesight is keen, and she knits constantly and rapidly—in the dark.

Edith, my sister, was born in Davenport but lived most of her life in Cedar Rapids where she attended Adams, McKinley, and old Washington schools. She was my dance partner in our teens and a musician besides. She plays the piano and sings in six languages. She was a Coe College student, class of 1939, until she left school to marry Robert M. Atkinson. For many years, she worked for Collins Radio.

Different Flies

We're still flies in the buttermilk since we're the only black couple in our neighborhood. But things are definitely different. Now instead of catering and entertaining at parties for the Elks or the Lions, we're catered to and entertained. Now instead of cleaning the town's bank buildings, I'm chairman of the Mark Twain Bank's Advisory Board, which designs methods and policies on how to serve elderly clients better. As a result of the board's work, the bank started a monthly newsletter with useful information, such as the best rates on CDs. They sponsor fashion shows and have speakers on health, exercise, and nutrition for older people. They hold golf competitions with golf pros to coach us. They have a special contact person for elderly customers. And they hold social events for all the bank's branches: dances, Christmas parties, and trips to caves, stage shows, and horse and dog racetracks.

Most of the board members are retired professionals with lots of power. It's an association of older people who have already made it. It's easy to experience real friendship with them because there's no pretense, no energy wasted on rivalry. One member picks wild berries, makes them into jelly, and brings them to us each year. Another eighty-year-old who worked for the telephone company for years is very good at logistics, so he puts together trips to Las Vegas and other places. A man who's good at photography has a camcorder and takes pictures of all our activities. Sportscaster Bill Grigsby tells great stories and keeps us in touch with civic news. He runs the city development commission and really knows what's going on. So they're all sharing their expertise and making life better for all of us.

One activity Evelyn and I particularly enjoy is the Baton Club because we both love music. We go to the meetings before the symphony in which the conductor explains what we're going to hear. Learning more about the music on the program makes it a greater treat. Besides, Evelyn likes to get dressed up, and I don't mind that either.

Other Differences

Things are different, too, when I travel these days. I stay in the best hotels in the country. When you travel with the government, as I did for so many years, you don't go first class. And there are other differences: in the old days I had to come in the backdoor of the beautiful hotels. Now, they roll out the red carpet and put me in their best suite—and that's all over the country, north and south.

When I first started speaking on my own, I was a little wary of some places, especially in the South. Then an associate asked me to speak to the National Electrical Contractors' Association because he said it could soothe old wounds and open new doors. I accepted, and they asked our wives to come, too. They treated us to a fancy dinner, and I was feeling quite relaxed. But later, when I walked into the hall to give my speech, I noticed the audience was totally white. When I finished speaking, everyone leapt to their feet in unison . . . and I cried. The man who introduced me said, "I'm going to do something I have never done before. I'm gonna hug a black man . . . this black man." After that, I went all over the country and spoke in all ten of the association's regions.

But there are still times when I feel "in harm's way" . . . still times when I'm embarrassed. Recently, I was paying my bill in a fine hotel. I presented my lifetime credit card which can be used anywhere in the hotel. The cashier looked surprised and asked, "Where did you get this? I thought these cards were for *executives*." She assumed that a black man couldn't be an executive. I didn't make a fuss, but I did report it to the hotel manager.

Sometimes those things are just funny to me. Once I was at the airport in Memphis, Tennessee, dressed pretty nice, I thought, in a white jacket and dark trousers. A white guy in a wheelchair called to me, "Hey, boy, would you roll me down to the gate?" I said, "Sure," and took him down. He gave me a $5 tip. I put it in the Salvation Army Christmas pot. I would have done it for him free because I was going that way, but I thought, "Why not take the money for a good purpose?"

Another time, I was invited to Des Moines to speak to a religious group. After I got settled in my hotel room, I changed into jeans because I had noticed the kids in the hotel had on jeans and looked so comfortable in them. This woman came up to me and said, "Move these chairs over there." I wasn't doing anything, so I moved them for her. Then she said, "We need another table over here." I said, "I don't know where the tables are." She was plainly irritated and said in kind of a threatening way, "I'm going to call the manager." I laughed and said, "That's a good idea, I don't work here, so I can't help you anymore." She was really embarrassed.

There's still some unconscious or unintentional discrimination at times. It's so subtle, I can't be sure it's true. I feel it sometimes with the airlines when the person who collects the boarding passes reaches around me to take tickets from the people behind me. One once said, "You're not in line," but there was no one behind me. Sometimes the flight attendant greets everyone else with a smile and hello but looks the other way when I show up. Sometimes the plane is loaded, but you're seated by yourself. Or sometimes you're sitting in a row with all blacks. You ask for an upgrade using your frequent flier points, and they say the flight is full. Then you find there are only three or four people in first class. I don't make a lot of noise and argue with them. But I do report it to their manager or supervisor in a call or letter. Whether it's discrimination or not, it's poor customer service, and management needs to know about it.

Lessons Learned

As I look back over the many experiences I've had, I'm amazed at some of the changes that have occurred in my lifetime . . . most of them for the good. I've learned a few things along the way that might seem kind of simple to some folks, but I agree with Robert Fulghum's attitude: "All I really need to know I learned in kindergarten." In other words, the simple lessons are the truest and most useful. So here are a few of my "learnings." Some I've mentioned before in the book, but I think they bear repeating. These lessons apply to everyone, but a few are especially for blacks and other minorities.

Even though I have lectured at many universities and colleges (this photo was taken at Nebraska Central College's commencement program), my formal schooling consists of high school and college-level correspondence classes. I was born fifty years after slavery was abolished and grew up through two wars and the Great Depression. My folks had a home that encouraged a love of learning through work and reading. Ev and I have always had a home filled with books, and these days I have the time to read almost as much as I've always wanted—approximately two books a week.

Don't stay too close to where you got into bed. A preacher friend of mine told about the time his little boy fell out of bed. When his father asked what happened, the boy said, "I guess I stayed too close to where I got in." Living in black sections does not prepare blacks and other minorities for the real world—nor the real world for them. Instead of clinging to the homes and businesses we have in black sections, we need to keep what we have and move onward or we'll soon be in retreat.

Constant upkeep and new strategies are needed to maintain advances during changing conditions. Since the time of Martin Luther King, Jr., many of the gains have been lost through neglect. Blacks need to push into the larger community. Join white clubs, move to white neighborhoods, go to white churches. The music won't be as good and you'll feel uncomfortable for a while, but think what you'll be doing for your country.

This decade is ripe for blacks to capitalize upon the gains made since 1955. I foresee a black in the White House soon, perhaps even in my lifetime (I'm planning on another twenty years). My prescription: we need more flies in the buttermilk to the point where blacks and other minorities are present in every segment of our society.

Take your role models where you find them. Blacks often say, "We don't have role models." Don't limit yourself. Look around you and see who's made it. No matter what color they are, model yourself after them. I've had plenty of white role models in my life. If I'd waited for a black to come along, I'd have missed many opportunities to learn and advance, and I'd have missed some truly wonderful friendships. This applies to people born into poor or uneducated families. Find someone outside your family to speak, work, and behave like. You can work yourself out of poverty and ignorance by imitating someone you admire.

Pick your moments to be bold. In the early days, blacks had to walk a fine line between courage and cowardice. There is more margin for error today, but there is still no point in thoughtless, extreme acts. There are times when it is just plain foolish to be bold. As the old saying goes, "There are old blacks, and bold blacks. But I've never seen any *old* bold blacks." Spend your courage and energy on situations that count.

Care about all people, not just your own. When I began to care about people in general, those other than blacks and my own family, everything began to come to me easily. Until then, I was handicapped by my concern for my own family and for survival. Once I let go of this limitation, everything seemed easier and more rewarding. This shift in point of view taught me, too, that you often get what you want when you least expect it. It reminds me of this quotation: "Happiness is like a butterfly. The more you chase it, the more it will elude you. But if you turn your attention to other things, it comes and softly sits on your shoulder."

Pay your "civic rent." W.G. used to talk about civic rent, the things you do and the money you give to support good works in the community. Well, part of the civic rent I like to pay goes to groups like the City Union Mission and Jackson County Temporary Housing. I know it helps people. Some nights I can't sleep from worrying about the people who live under the streets in New York and Chicago, about the thousands of sick, sad men, women, and children who wander the streets and countryside without a home, food, or friends. Even if you don't have money to give, you can pay your rent through community service. Give a helping hand whenever you can, and you'll keep up with your civic debt.

Don't jump from balconies when you're eighteen. Think about the impact your every action will have a few years from now. It's like the frill I added to the tap-dance routine I performed when I was eighteen. We did a good act for the white audiences, and they loved it. But when we performed for blacks, we went all out. We'd add all kinds of stunts just to outdo each other. When Edie and Wally and I were dancing for black audiences, we wore extra-flashy costumes, and I'd jump from the balcony onto the stage and land in a split!

For years I had trouble with my back, and I finally went to a chiropractor. He said my spine was all out of whack, and he wanted to know what I'd done to get it that way. I said I didn't know, but it had been that way ever since the balcony jumps. He seemed kind of amused and told me to stop doing them. Of course, I was middle-aged at that point and hadn't danced in a while, so I promised I'd follow doctor's orders. I was lucky that I just needed that one treatment to get my back straightened up. Some of the things you do when you're young, on a dare or to impress others, can cause you trouble the rest of your life.

What you're doing now affects you at forty-five and sixty. Smoking, drinking, overeating, jumping off balconies—is the pleasure of being cool today worth gasping for breath at fifty or having brain damage at sixty?

Take responsibility for everything you do. The old values kept us from chaos. We need to bring back respect for property and the rights of others. We need to expect good behavior from our children—and get it. Research shows that 80 percent of job applicants do not speak good English. I'm particularly bothered when blacks don't use the King's English. I have little patience with rapping and street talk in schools and the business world. If you talk that way at a Saturday night social, it's your business. But when you mispronounce words and use slang in the white world, you're hurting all blacks.

Monitor your actions; think how they're affecting others. Young people need to take stock of themselves, especially in regard to parenting. I hear about teenage girls having babies so they'll have someone to love. But think of the babies. They can't live on love, and you're trapping your baby and yourself in poverty by having children too early in life. Teenage boys brag about getting a girl pregnant. They think it's macho. Jesse Jackson is so right when he says, "A boy can make a baby, but it takes a man to raise one."

Words will never hurt me—don't you believe it. When we label people, when we call them names, we hurt them in a way that can't ever be fixed. The injuries of verbal abuse and violence become ugly wounds that spread infection throughout the whole body and sicken the soul. Verbal violence causes gentle children to grow into bitter, tortured adults. It turns self-esteem into self-hate, sometimes ending in self-destruction. Other times these victims of verbal abuse turn upon others and make war upon our society. It is said that most of the people in prison were abused children.

I'm glad to see that the National Center for the Prevention of Child Abuse is waging an advertising campaign with the slogan "Words Hurt." These ads point out that calling children names scars them emotionally. Adults need to be aware that just calling your child "skinny," "shorty," or "tubby" can hurt a child's self-esteem. And the meaner the name, the more damaging it is. Please think before you label your children or anyone else. Words have great power; use them with care.

Learn first what is easiest for you. Having an early success makes you want to do more. Then, too, you have some knowledge to build upon, which makes the next step a little easier. I think we should apply this idea to dropouts and poor students: give them small tasks they can accomplish easily instead of setting goals too high. For example, one of the largest airlines has its data-entry work performed by Taiwanese who cannot read English but just copy what they see. Why couldn't our dropouts perform such work? At least they understand the language. Rather than make them finish a course in typing or business English, just teach them to copy what they see. This would get them working and would build their confidence and skills. And we'd keep the jobs in the United States. You can turn this idea around when you're looking for a job. If you're not a full-range mechanic, apply for one part of repairs that you can master quickly, such as brakes or tire changes. You'll make wages in the mechanic range and be learning new skills watching others. You can get started in a field with a future.

When making a change, do a bit of bracing first. Touch everyone you can in and around the system that you want to change. People need to be prepared a little. It'll be easier for everyone involved—and the change will turn out better.

In your work, be unique, do something extra. Work is important to every part of your life. Be smart in the way you handle it. Whether you are in your own business or just trying to get ahead on the job, find a way to be unique, to go the extra mile. Work is more satisfying when you add your special touch . . . and you'll also be more successful. I always took every job I had and treated it as though it were my own business. That way, I had control over even the worst, messiest task. I took pride in doing it the very best I knew how . . . in finding a better way of doing a dirty job. That way, it was never unbearable.

When you're looking for work, take jobs that no one else wants, and do them well. There have been times in my life when I've had little choice. But when you do a tough job well, you get the attention and admiration of others. Furthermore, you'll eventually make pretty good money. Others will be glad they don't have to do it and be happy to pay for it.

Politeness is contagious. My folks brought us up to be polite, and we always were. When you treat people in a civil way, they are civil in return. It sounds kind of phony on paper, but in person it really works. When someone is upset or complaining to you, listen and respond in a polite way. Their emotions will calm, and reason will reign.

It's even more important in groups. I learned in the state legislature how politeness helps when you're trying to get something done. The intensity of a situation seems to pick up momentum as the number of people involved increases. People in groups can get very hostile or be very formal and polite. It's much safer and more effective to have the germ of good manners infect your life than spreading negative words and feelings.

A Last Word

If I had to sum up all the lessons I've learned in my long, busy life, I guess I'd have to say the most important one came to me gradually. In the early years, life was a constant struggle to stay afloat in the buttermilk. But as I traveled and spoke to more and more audiences, I realized that life is really an opportunity to learn about others and care about what happens to them.

Since then, my life has been not as a fly in the buttermilk but more like a passenger on an airplane ride. When trouble or turbulence comes, you listen to the pilot and fasten your seatbelt while you move above it . . . to 20,000 feet. Use that problem as an educational experience. When the turbulence comes again, fasten your seatbelt and move up to 30,000 feet where it's even smoother and less confining.

Then, when you hit another rough spot, rise on up again . . . up . . . up . . . to 38,000 feet. When you get up there, seven miles high, you suddenly break through to where it's smooth and bright. No more fear, no more fly in the buttermilk. Now I'm flying above it. Free now, above the clouds. Free to look down and see our beautiful country so rich in diversity. Free to continue an endless mission to bring about harmony in a world of difference.

Singular Lives